WHAT WENT WRONG WITH
ECONOMICS

THE FLAWED ASSUMPTIONS
THAT LED ECONOMISTS ASTRAY

Michael Reiss PhD

Goldhurst Press
London

Contents

Contents

Contents

Preface: Economics, It's Not Rocket Science... Is It?

Brain surgery, higher mathematics, quantum mechanics; everyone knows they're hard. If you ask someone in the street for their opinion on those disciplines, the most likely answer is: "I haven't got a clue, leave it to the experts." Very few people are embarrassed to admit that they know little of such things. Economics, however, does not appear to be in that category. Economics seems to have a characteristic it shares with driving skill. Surveys of drivers show that the majority of people think that they are more skilled than the average. On the surface, running an economy does not appear to be so difficult. If we all work hard, get the unions out of the way, have low taxes and invest in industry, the economy should get along just fine. It's all just common sense, isn't it?

The evidence would suggest that there is something wrong with this view. The economy appears to do crazy things. There are wild booms and busts, periods of seemingly out-of-control inflation and other periods of high unemployment. The busts are often not predicted, even by the most esteemed economists. Indeed a report produced by the International Monetary Fund concluded that the world economy was in great shape in April 2007 only for the biggest economic crash since the Great Depression to happen just months later.

A symptom of this "it's all just common sense" attitude towards economics is that the most unlikely people are selected to run the economy in various countries around the world. People who have shown little sign of mathematical or scientific prowess are selected on the basis that they are good, honest people, or they are great orators, or they ran a successful business. Looking at the academic backgrounds of the past ten people placed in charge of the British economy in recent years, we find that only three of them had some degree level training in economics and the remaining seven had the following backgrounds:

Chancellor	Main subject at degree level or higher
George Osborne	History
Alistair Darling	Law
Gordon Brown	History
Kenneth Clarke	Law
John Major	None (left school at 16)
Geoffrey Howe	Law
Denis Healey	Classics

It should be noted that none of the ten had any degree level education in mathematics, physics, engineering or any other hard science.

Just at the time of writing a new politician, Alan Johnson, has just been selected by the leader of the main opposition party in the UK to be the shadow chancellor. It is interesting to note his credentials. He left school at 15 (even earlier than John Major), then stacked shelves in a supermarket before progressing to become a postman at age 18. If the position of "head of brain surgery" at a major hospital became vacant then there is no way Alan would even get an interview, let alone the job. But somehow, for the post of "head of economics", Alan is deemed suitable.

So what is it within economics that trips people up? What features of it lead politicians and bankers to get things so badly wrong time and time again? The answer is that it's not "common" sense at all. Economics is deceptively hard. There are several counter-intuitive aspects of our economic system that are either not widely known or are generally misunderstood. Most, if not all, university-level economics textbooks have inadequate, out-of-date or misleading information about a variety of critically important phenomena:

- fractional reserve banking (ill-understood/ignored)
- Keynesian beauty contests and their consequences (largely ignored)
- Ponzi dynamics in asset pricing (largely ignored)
- the paradox of thrift (ill-understood)
- inflation (ill-understood)
- the invisible hand (overestimated powers).

Hopefully by the end if this book you will have a good grasp of all of these things and will be in a position to understand our economic situation better than many professional economists.

A quick test: If you know someone that claims to know about economics and you are uncertain as to whether they really do or not, then try this test on them: Ask them to explain how money gets created *and destroyed* by the banks. If they cannot do so, then it is inconceivable that they could properly understand our current economic situation.

1 Our Crazy Money System

This chapter will explain the basic money creation/destruction mechanism, both in theory and in practice.

"It's a process that, even today, few bankers understand" – Milton Friedman – Nobel Prize winner in economics, 1976.

Misconceptions about money

A few misconceptions about money and how much of it exists are worth considering. This is what most non-economists would assume:

> **"There's a sum of money floating around in the economy, and people use it as a medium of exchange. The total amount of money out there is approximately fixed."**

Some people may have thought about inflation a little and may perhaps have a more sophisticated notion like:

> **"There's a sum of money floating around in the economy, and people use it as a medium of exchange. The total amount of money out there would be constant**

> **except that the government regularly prints more of it, a few per cent extra per year, so the total amount of money in the economy only ever goes up."**

... and many people would be quite certain of this:

> **"Only the government has the power to increase the amount of money in the economy."**

None of these statements are true however, and without a good grasp of the truth about money creation and, very importantly, destruction, you have little chance of understanding economics. Having said that, it is remarkable that so many economists treat the money creation mechanism as a "technical detail" that is learned superficially and inaccurately at the start of an economics degree and then promptly forgotten about or disregarded forever more.

The creation and destruction mechanism is in fact rather strange and its widespread misunderstanding among the majority of economists is one of the main reasons that the economics profession has such a poor reputation among the sciences.

So let's fix this right now and explain how money works:

The money system used throughout the world in modern times has evolved from something called *fractional reserve banking.* The way that this gets taught in most textbooks is significantly different to how the system works in practice but the textbook explanation is a perfectly good place to start. We shall explain this first and then point out the "real-world corrections" afterwards. Doing it this way will also give you an insight into how many economists are mistaken in their understanding of money.

Fractional reserve banking (as told in the textbooks)

When people "store" their money in banks, they know full well that the banks may use some of it to lend out to other people. This immediately begs the question: "What happens if I want to take all my money out again at short notice?" The answer is that the banks never lend out *all* your money, they keep some in reserve. So if you want to take it all out then the bank can give you back that fraction of your money that they didn't lend out, with the remainder made up from the pool of un-lent-out parts of everyone else's accounts. This then begs another question: "What happens if *all* (or a large fraction) of the customers come to take out all their money at the same time?" This possibility is known as a *bank run*. The answer is that the bank then has a big problem. It will not have enough money to pay out to all its customers. This is a serious situation, and to make this unlikely, governments over the years have tried a variety of schemes, the exact choice of which has profound implications for the whole economy. One way of doing this is for the government to make rules about exactly what fraction of people's savings the banks must keep in reserve. The larger the fraction the less likely that the bank will ever be in a position where it does not have enough money in store to give to customers asking to withdraw their money. This fraction is known as the *reserve requirement*.

In our modern society, most of the money that we have to our names is not stored as a pile of cash under the mattress; instead almost all of it is in the bank. If someone handed you $100,000 in cash in the street, then (after you'd got over the surprise of being handed $100,000!) you'd probably feel very nervous carrying so much cash and be very keen to get that money to the bank as soon as possible in case you got mugged. You'd feel much more comfortable knowing that you had that money in the bank but that you were armed with a cheque book (or credit/debit card – a more modern equivalent) that enabled you to spend your money in dribs and drabs as and when you needed it. Keep this in mind as we consider the following:

Let's say that the reserve requirement is 10% (a fraction often quoted in economics textbooks). Let's also imagine that the world's first ever bank has just opened up and their very first customer (Man

A) comes in with $1,000 cash to deposit for safe-keeping. The bank would give him a cheque book and make a note on its computers that he can spend up to $1,000 with his cheques. Note that Man A can now spend up to $1,000 with his cheques.

Then a second customer (Man B) comes in wanting to borrow $900 (the maximum the reserve requirement allows the bank to lend out) in order for him to buy a used car. The borrower typically does not take out any cash; instead the bank just gives the borrower a cheque book and makes a note on its computers of the fact that the borrower is allowed to spend up to $900 with his cheques. Note that the bank still has the original $1,000 cash in its vaults.

Now:

Man A can spend up to $1,000 with his cheques

and

Man B can spend up to $900 with his cheques.

The "spending power" of the community at large has grown by $900.

Now the borrower goes to buy his car from Man C. He writes out a cheque for $900 and hands it over. Man B no longer has any money to spend. Indeed over the coming months or years he will gradually have to pay back the loan plus interest in instalments, but at the moment we are just considering the short term. Man C can now go to the bank and start up a new account. He stores (deposits) his $900 cheque and walks out with his own cheque book, the bank having noted that he is allowed to spend up to $900.

Now:

Man A can spend up to $1,000 with his cheques

and

Man C can spend up to $900 with his cheques.

Now this is where the craziness starts… The bank is then allowed to treat that $900 cheque as a new deposit and is allowed to lend out 90% (or $810) of *that*. The bank may lend it to Man D…

Now:

Man A can spend up to $1,000 with his cheques

and

Man C can spend up to $900 with his cheques

and

Man D can spend up to $810 with his cheques.

This process can repeat itself over and over, starting with a loan of $900 then $810 then $729 then $656.10 and so on and so on in an ever decreasing sequence. This can all happen because, with the use of cheques, the original $1,000 cash does not need to be touched; it can just sit there in the bank. The original $1,000 has been transformed into a series of cheques that can be used as a medium of exchange. These cheques behave as, and indeed are, real money. The sum total of this series of cheques turns out to be $10,000. This may seem like a strangely round number, but that's just the way the maths turns out.

Figure 1-1 The effects of fractional reserve banking.

As you can now see, fractional reserve banking is a system in which $10,000 of "money" can be created from a starting base of $1,000.

The story told so far has left out all sorts of complications, like there being more than one bank, interest being charged on loans and many other factors, but none of these complications alters the essential conclusion: **The total amount of money (cash + cheques + other "electronic money") available for society to spend can be a large multiple of the total amount of "real" money the system starts with.**

Some people when first shown a description of fractional reserve banking assume it must be some mathematical sleight of hand, or perhaps some kind of conspiracy theory that the mainstream economists would dispute. But what has been described so far is not at all contentious, it is simply not widely known among the general public, or most politicians for that matter.

Some definitions: The $1,000 in the above story is part of what is known as the *monetary base* while the $10,000 is part of what is called the *money supply*. The "money" that can be spent with checks is sometimes referred to as *cheque book money*. The type of bank account described in this story is known as a *demand deposit*.

Fractional reserve banking, in reality

Fractional reserve banking is used all around the world today, but it doesn't work quite as described in the textbooks. The textbooks tell a story which implies that the reserve ratio puts a hard limit on the total amount of money that can be lent out. The key error in the textbooks is the idea that money cannot be lent out if it would break the reserve requirement limits even for a second. The truth in the real world, however, is that the "limits" are intended to be enforced *on average* over an extended period, often a couple of weeks. The result is that loans can be made which break the limits temporarily and then the banks can seek out the money to comply with requirements later. The process of making the loans produces more money than is required for the reserves. So when the borrower spends the money it will come back to the banking sector, guaranteeing that some institutions will be in possession of excess reserves. This means that any banks that are short can seek out others with an excess and borrow the money in order to comply. The result of this process is that the reserve requirements are not a restriction on money creation at all. Remarkably few economists are aware of this leak in the system but it most certainly does exist and some very senior people right at the heart of the banking system are indeed aware of it.

The textbook description of fractional reserve banking is wrong

Any claim that all the textbooks have it wrong needs some strong evidence to back it up. So here is a selection…

In his book *Towards True Monetarism* Geoffrey Gardiner states:

> Conventional textbook theory needs a slight clarification. Popular textbooks even modern ones seem to imply that there can be shortages of funds in which the Bank of England can supply only by creating new money. There authors may have somewhat misinterpreted the practicalities of the situation through incomplete mastery of the principles of double entry book keeping. They failed to see that all money is debt and that if debt has been created by a bank the money for a balancing deposit has inevitably been created too. Any funds needed to eliminate a shortage must already be on their way to the Bank of England because any surplus must show up in the books once the system's brief time-lag has been overcome. A permanent creation of new money should therefore never be necessary. Judging by their private statements bank treasurers well understand this principle.

He adds:

> In a lecture the head of treasury operations of a large clearing bank was most emphatic: "If we are short of funds we know they have to be around somewhere: it is just a question of finding where they are and then paying the price to get them."

Professor Steve Keen wrote:

> Basil Moore is the venerable father of the proposition that the money supply is endogenously determined, rather than set exogenously by the Central Bank, as is still taught (in wild conflict with both the empirical data and actual Central Bank knowledge and practice) in almost all macroeconomics courses.

"Understanding the Remarkable Survival of Multiplier Models of Money Stock Determination" by Seth B. Carpenter and Selva Demiralp. Published on the Federal Reserve's own website!

Another factor usually unreported in the textbooks is that the reserve requirements have been diminishing over the years. Often they vary according to the types of loan, with some types having zero requirement. Many countries have simply abandoned statutory reserve requirements altogether and just leave it to the banks to decide for themselves how much to hold in reserve.

Capital adequacy

The supposed "restrictions" on money creation are now controlled by a new system called the *capital adequacy ratio*. This is a requirement that a bank is the owner of a certain collection of assets (known as the *equity capital reserve*) as a fraction of its loans. The composition of the types of asset that a bank is required to possess and the methods prescribed for determining their value are subject to a whole raft of ever-changing rules and regulations.

Given the fact that the old reserve ratio system did not limit lending in any way, you may be wondering whether capital adequacy fairs any better? Sadly the answer is no. For a start, banks can sidestep their rules with some accounting trickery.

Professor Charles Goodhart, a former member of the Monetary Policy Committee for the Bank of England, said in a recent television interview: "A lot of very clever people [who] were hired by banks with very large salaries worked for months to try and find very clever and ingenious and legal ways to get around the regulations." The accounting tricks they came up with have been documented in many other books so we won't go into any detail here, but the gist of the most common trick involved a process known as *securitisation* which works as follows:

Bank X makes a loan of $500,000 to Miss Jones for her to buy a house, thereby creating $500,000 of new money. Imagine that after having made this loan the bank is now right on the limits of how much it is allowed to lend out according to the capital adequacy rules. Now the bank is barred from making any more loans unless it purchases some more assets. But now it can "sell" the loan. The idea of selling a loan may seem a little strange, but remember that the loan is effectively an IOU from Miss Jones stating that she will pay back $500,000 plus interest over some period. This IOU is valuable and can be sold on to someone else. If some third party comes along and purchases the loan from Bank X then Bank X can claim that the loan has effectively (according to the strict letter of the capital adequacy rules) been "repaid" and so it is now free to make another loan without having to purchase any more capital. Notice that the $500,000 of new money has leaked out into the system. The capital adequacy rules have not placed any limit on money creation.

The conclusion from looking at the way reserve ratios and capital adequacy work in practice is that there is no limit at all on the amount of money that banks can create other than their ability to find people they can lend to and make a profit from.

Characteristics of our banking system

Some may be thinking that perhaps the current monetary system is just too complicated for it to be worth putting in the effort to understand it unless you are training to be a banker. Surely it's just a collection of boring technical details. Surely real-world, day-to-day economics can be understood perfectly well without paying attention to the monetary system. Unfortunately this is not the case. The millions of people who have lost their jobs around the world following the 2007/8 crash have lost their jobs very largely because of politicians', and even central bankers', failure to understand the behaviour of their own monetary system. This chapter will not go into the complex details of the rules and regulations (that could fill a large book by itself) but instead will try to convey simply the important characteristics of the system:

Money can disappear!

You will notice that in the description of fractional reserve banking, additional money gets created by the banks when they lend to people. The converse is also true, i.e. **when people pay back their loans the money disappears.**

Indeed in the lending and relending scenario described at the start of this chapter, if nobody else borrowed any more money and all that happened was that the borrowers gradually paid back their loans, the total amount of money in the system would shrink back down from $10,000 to $1,000. The idea of the total amount of money in an economy reducing may seem a little odd, but it does certainly happen. All that is required is for there to be a mass reluctance to borrow and the money supply will decrease as the existing loans are paid back.

The most dramatic example of a shrinking money supply was possibly that which occurred during the Great Depression. During that period the money supply in the US diminished by around one third. Unfortunately there are unpleasant consequences of a shrinking money supply and governments may take actions to try to avoid it. So historically big reductions are relatively rare. Sadly the actions that governments may take to prevent these reductions can also have bad effects as we shall see later.

Money disappearing? That sounds crazy!

The concept of money disappearing sounds so strange that some people have trouble believing it. We would like to assure you that among monetary economists this idea is not at all contentious. To help appreciate why money should disappear, consider the following: Borrowing money from a bank can be considered as an exchange of IOUs. The IOU the borrower gives to the bank is the loan agreement with the borrower's signature on it. The IOU the bank gives to the borrower is the cheque book money. Cheque book money can be seen as a spendable IOU from the bank. When the loan is repaid, the two IOUs simply cancel each other out. They will both cease to exist.

This does not mean that real paper money needs to be torn up or burned. If the borrower pays back their loan in paper money, then the bank will simply remove the equivalent amount of *electronic* money within its computer systems.

Ballooning and shrinking

Hopefully you can see now that this potential ballooning and possible shrinking of the total amount of money in the economy by a very large factor could have a dramatic effect on how economies work. Indeed it is the ballooning and shrinking of the money supply that has dominated all the major financial crises since fractional reserve banking was invented. This issue shall be examined again in later chapters.

An ill-understood, ramshackle system

You might imagine that the reserve ratio and other regulatory requirements are well understood by virtually anyone that calls themselves an economist. Unfortunately this could not be further from the truth. It would be more accurate to say that the reserve ratio and the other rules governing bank lending are a ramshackle, arcane, ever-changing collection of regulations that get tweaked, botched and fiddled with as the banking industry limps from crisis to crisis.

The information about how it all works is very hard to come by. Any description of the system you find in economic textbooks is almost certainly out of date and was probably incorrect and/or woefully incomplete at the time of its printing. Just as one example, the 848-page *Principles of Economics* by N. Gregory Mankiw (third edition), one of the most popular standard economics textbooks sold in the world today, has a section on "The Monetary System" which makes no mention of the fact that the reserve requirements vary depending on the type of account, and makes no mention of the capital adequacy ratio at all. It does have a short section entitled "Problems in Controlling the Money Supply" which contains the following sentences:

> Yet, if the Fed is vigilant, these problems need not be large. The Fed collects data on the deposits and reserves from the banks every week, so it is quickly aware of any changes in depositor or banker behaviour. It can, therefore, respond to these changes and keep the money supply close to whatever it chooses.

These soothing words give the impression that everything is under control. Any student reading this book is hardly likely to take any special interest in the money supply when it appears to be such a boring, stable beast. This attitude appears to be the orthodoxy in economics teaching. The textbooks may as well write: "The control of the money supply is a boring technical issue, please ignore."

Now contrast this sentiment with the sight of Hank Paulson (the US treasury secretary at the time) metaphorically putting a gun to the head of Congress on the weekend of the 27/28 September 2008 and saying if you don't create $700 billion of new money to give to the banking sector by Monday morning then the US economy will collapse. The behaviour, side-effects and control of the money supply are perhaps *the* most important things any economist could possibly study and it is about time standard economic textbooks reflected this fact.

You would expect that information on the current rules and regulations about money creation would all be public knowledge. You may think there would be websites that explain it all in plain English, but there are no such things. There are some web pages on the sites of some banks, but as with the economics textbooks, the information is woefully inadequate and/or out of date; usually both.

But what about the interest?

One question remains around the lending and repayment of money: What about the interest payments? The answer is that when a loan gets paid back, the original money created by the loan disappears, but the bank is allowed to keep the interest repayments. This is how banks get their income.

Some people, when presented with this information about how the banking system works, become concerned about where the supply of money for interest payments could possibly come from. They say things like: "If the total size of the money supply was fixed then there is no possible source of money for paying interest." This may be followed by: "So this proves that the money supply is forced to increase forever, otherwise borrowers could never pay the money back." They suspect that a proportion of borrowers must on aggregate, almost by definition, be unable to repay the interest. This view is however, mistaken. Indeed Professor Steve Keen of the University of Western Sydney has recently produced computer simulations to prove it. The key thing to note is that the interest paid does not simply accumulate at the bank. The interest is shared between the bank's owners, employees and savers, all of whom will be spending their earned interest back into the economy. This flow of money is a source of money for the interest payments.

The supposed impossibility of repaying interest is bit like the following dilemma. Imagine two people on a desert island: Mary and Sue. Sue owes Mary $20 but there are only $10 in existence and this is currently in the hands of Mary. At first glance it appears that the debt could never be repaid but this apparent impasse is easily solved. All that has to happen is for Sue to sell Mary some good or service. Say, for example, Sue spends some hours catching fish. She could sell the fish to Mary for $10. This $10 could then immediately be given back to Mary as part payment for the debt. Now simply repeat the process one more time and the debt is cleared. The total amount of money that can be paid by Person A to Person B is *not* limited by the total amount of money that exists in an economy.

Sadly Steve Keen's proof of the repayability of interest is not widely known and it is all too common for both economists and politicians to assume that it is essential for the money supply to continuously grow in order for an economy to function.

The fact that there is no in-built mathematical paradox to avoid when paying back interest does not necessarily guarantee that all loans will be paid back; far from it. If someone borrows a large a sum on the basis that they expect healthy future income to repay the interest there is always scope for things to go wrong. They may lose their job, or they may become ill; perhaps their business plan was flawed and the product they are making proves unpopular. Any of these problems may lead to a situation where the loan repayments are larger than the borrower can ever reasonably pay back. This is possible even if the loan was interest free.

In conclusion we can now see that it is not essential for the money supply to grow in order for interest payments to be made on loans without defaults. There are a variety of problems caused by fractional reserve banking, some of them severe (as we shall see later), but inherently unpayable interest is not one of them.

How old is our monetary system?

Many people assume that the way our monetary and banking systems works is many hundreds of years old and so its faults and foibles must have had plenty of time to be understood and problems ironed out. Indeed some aspects of the system are hundreds of years old but, depending on how you define our "current system", it's truer to say that it has only been around since 1971 at the earliest. Before that time the money supply was constrained by a guarantee that the government would exchange a certain quantity of gold for each dollar. But since 1971, when Richard Nixon removed that guarantee from the US dollar, most currencies worldwide have been backed by nothing at all. A currency backed by nothing is called a *fiat currency*, fiat meaning "by decree".

So 1971 was perhaps the last fundamental change, but there have been more recent changes that are still very significant, like the "Basel" I and II sets of regulations, agreed in 1988 and 2004 respectively, and a major repeal of regulations made under the Clinton administration in 1999. It makes you wonder then how bankers manage to have such an "establishment" image when what they are doing should really be considered as an experiment that's only just got underway.

It is not much of an exaggeration to say that the history of economics has been a history of mankind's attempts, and mostly dismal failures, at establishing and sustaining a stable monetary system. Since money was invented, literally thousands of currencies have failed. This tit-bit of information is not generally published in the standard economics textbooks.

Can you have a fixed money supply system?

The short answer is yes. Though almost never discussed in modern mainstream economics textbooks, there are economists who have devoted a lot of time and effort to designing monetary systems without the ballooning and shrinking characteristics of fractional reserve banking. After the collapse that led to the Great Depression there was for a while some serious consideration of an alternative monetary system known as *100% reserve banking*. There are many subtle variations of this system that have been proposed over the years, most notably by Irving Fisher in his 1935 book *100% Money*. In more modern times, a similar system was proposed by Nobel-Prize-winning economist Milton Friedman. This section will give only the basic outline of a 100% reserve system.

Before we can introduce such a system, we must first consider the contradiction which lies at the heart of fractional reserve banking. It is easy to do this by just considering the very first loan of the possible sequence of loans discussed in the previous sections:

A bank has just opened up and their first customer, Man A, has just deposited $1,000 cash for safe-keeping. Man B then comes in asking to borrow $900. The bank gives Man B a cheque book and tells him he can now spend up to $900 using these cheques. The total money supply, or the total spending power of the economy, has now grown from $1,000 to $1,900.

Now consider this state of affairs from the point of view of the two men. Man A may think, "I have $1,000. I could go to the market today and buy $1,000 worth of stuff." At exactly the same time, Man B may be thinking, "I have $900. I could go to the market today and buy $900 worth of stuff." Indeed they are both correct: they could both go to the market and spend all their money at the same time; the system would not break down in any way.

Now let's contrast this scenario with one in which banks did not exist. We start off with Man A having $1,000 and now Man B wants to borrow $900. Man B would have to ask if he could borrow the $900 directly from Man A. If the loan went ahead, look at the situation now. Man B, like before, may think to himself, "I have $900. I could go to the market today and buy $900 worth of stuff." But now look at the state of Man A. He will be thinking to himself: "I may have a net worth of $1,000, but right now I only have $100. If I go to the market today I could only buy $100 worth of stuff." This situation is clearly very different to the one with banks and cheques. The key difference is that without banks Man A is forced to accept that if he lends out his money, then, at least until the loan is repaid, he will have less money to spend. This is all perfectly reasonable. Man A can't possibly have any cause for complaint. He agreed to lend man B the $900, probably in return for an interest payment. The situation without banks is perfectly natural. It is the situation *with* banks and cheques that is unnatural. With fractional reserve banking, Man A can effectively lend out $900 and at the same moment still be able to spend it!

Any monetary system which did not expand the money supply would have to have the characteristic that when you lend money to someone, you cannot spend that money until it gets paid back. A simple way to achieve this is through something called *time deposits*.

Demand and time deposits in a 100% reserve system

Often people with money to spare may consider their wealth as divisible into two parts: 1) day-to-day spending money that they may wish to call upon at very short notice, and 2) money they are saving up for some longer-term purpose. What they can do is give the "day-to-day" money to a bank and say, "Keep this safe for me, but don't lend it to anyone because I may need to spend it at any time." They could not reasonably expect to gain any interest on this money, as the bank has no way to profit from it. Indeed the customer may have to pay the bank for its trouble keeping it safe. This type of bank account falls within the existing definition of a *demand deposit* account, but in a 100% reserve system banks may *not* loan out this money.

The "long-term" money, however, could be given to a bank with the following, different set of instructions: "Here's some money I want you to lend out to other people so that it can earn interest. I promise to give you plenty of notice about when I need it back." This arrangement is known as a *time deposit*. The exact terms and conditions of what will be meant by "giving plenty of notice" are perhaps up for discussion. The purest form is that you absolutely cannot get your money back until you have served your notice. Other variations may state something like, "You can have your money back at short notice, but you have to pay a penalty for the privilege."

It should be immediately obvious that a system working with time deposits has enormous in-built protection against bank runs. It matters not one jot if the entire population want to take their "day-to-day" money out of the banks because none of it has been lent out to anyone else. If large numbers of people want to take out their "long-term" money, then exactly what happens depends on the terms and conditions of "giving plenty of notice". If the rules are that people could not have their money at all until the notice periods were served then there is no problem. The banks can simply insist that the customers wait for their loans to be paid back. If the rules are more flexible then there could indeed be a problem, but the very fact that there may be penalties involved in getting your money out "early" would mitigate against any such sudden wave of withdrawals. And besides, if the total money supply was no bigger (or not much bigger) than the original "base money" anyway, then the chances of a bank being unable to fulfil its customers' demands are dramatically reduced.

A mistake you may see in textbooks

Mainstream economists discuss 100% reserve banking so infrequently that misconceptions about it have crept into some textbooks. The classic mistake is the assumption that with 100% reserves banks cannot make loans from savers' money *at all*. Some economists have assumed that fractional reserve banking is simply the only way banking could possibly work. They have suggested that banks could not act as financial intermediaries between savers and borrowers without it. This is quite simply nonsense.

Why don't we use a fixed money supply system?

Clearly the fixed (or nearly fixed) money supply system as just described, has pros and cons compared to our current system. From the point of view of people who keep their money in banks, it appears to be a nuisance. The banks may quite rightly charge a fee for the safe-keeping of the "day-to-day" money and there is the irritating dilemma of having to always think hard about how long you are willing to allow your "long-term" money to be tied up. Compared to our current more flexible system, time deposits seem very clumsy. These inconveniences may however be a small price to pay when you start to look at the enormity of the problems associated with our current banking system. We will consider these in later chapters.

Summary

The precise rules and regulations covering money creation and destruction have been changing continuously, but for at least the period 1971 to the present we can make the following observations:

- Most new money gets created when it is lent out by banks.

- Money disappears when loans are paid back or defaulted on.

- The total money supply grows or shrinks according to the net balance between the following factors:

Increasing	new loans being taken out
	base money creation by governments
Decreasing	existing loans being paid back or defaulted on

Table 1-1 Factors that alter the money supply.

2 How Do Banks Go Bust?

With most failing businesses, the trigger for "going bust" is when one or more creditors demands payment that the company cannot fulfil. If the company cannot pay, then the creditors can go to a court and get the company wound up, forcing it to sell its assets in an attempt to pay off its debts. In the case of banks, however, they are "bust" almost by definition as soon as they start trading. If all their creditors (i.e. depositors) turned up demanding their money, the banks could not fulfil their demands. Judged by the same criteria as ordinary businesses, they would be "bankrupt" from the outset. For this reason, the government defines completely separate sets of rules for governing banks from those for governing any other type of business. There are special rules for determining when banks are deemed to have failed.

All countries have some kind of regulatory body whose job it is to monitor the bank's adherence to the rules about reserve requirements and/or capital adequacy ratios. If a bank falls short of these requirements then the regulator is supposed to force the bank to close. Its assets will then be sold off and the money used to pay off some of the bank's creditors. Often governments have a guarantee that the bank's depositors will not lose any of their savings, so the taxpayer may have to pay out to cover those losses.

At times of crisis, normal bank regulation may not apply

When an economic bubble bursts, the value of broad classes of assets can undergo precipitous falls. Banks may be holding on to large quantities of these assets in order to comply with their prescribed minimum capital adequacy ratios. The falling value of these assets may cause many banks to suddenly be in breach of their legal requirements. If the existing regulations were applied to the letter, this would mean forcing large numbers of banks to close simultaneously. This is perceived as being so catastrophic for the economy that governments often cannot bear for this to happen. At this point one of several possible strategies may be used:

1. **Take the bank into government ownership** (perhaps to be re-privatised at later date). The bank's shareholders would lose most, if not all, their money but the bank's customers would keep their deposits intact. This is essentially the plan carried out by the Swedish government after a property bubble burst in 1992.

2. **Bail out the bank.** If the bank is considered "too big to fail" then one possible action is for the government to simply give or lend the bank more money (possibly with strings attached) so that their reserve requirements or capital adequacy ratios are met. This "solution" to the problem may be very painful because the money used will have to come from the taxpayer. At the time of writing, the sums of money used to bail out the banks are so large that in several countries they correspond to many thousands of dollars per man, woman and child.

3. **Change the rules**, so that the bank is no longer in breach.

4. **Simply choose not to enforce the existing rules.**

Various combinations of 1 to 4 have been tried in different crises around the world. At the time of writing, after the 2007/8 crash the US government is applying a mixture of 2, 3 and 4. The "bail out" is common knowledge, but the rule changes and the non-enforcing of rules are less widely known.

As an example of 3: In April 2009, the Financial Accounting Standards Board (FASB) changed the accounting rules that determine the value of assets held by the banks. The old system, prescribed in the Basel II accord, was known as *mark to market*, which essentially states that assets can be valued according to the typical price that they are currently selling for on the open market. The FASB changed the system to something called *mark to model* in which assets are evaluated according to rather optimistic predictions of income from that asset in the future. This change has led to a significant increase in the recorded "value" of the assets held by the banks, making them more able to comply with the capital adequacy requirements.

As an example of 4: William K. Black, a former bank regulator, was asked about the Obama administration's handling of the financial sector in an interview for the *Bill Moyers Journal*. He replied:

> they [the government] violate the rule of law. This is being done just like Secretary Paulson did it. In violation of the law. We adopted a law after the Savings and Loan crisis, called the Prompt Corrective Action Law. And it requires them to close these institutions. And they're refusing...

In conclusion

In normal times, regulation works and small banks are allowed to fail if they breach their legal ratios. This is a process that helps weed out the badly run banks, leaving only the well run ones to survive. This policy is unlikely to be carried out if it would result in many banks failing simultaneously. Instead public money may be used to rescue the banks and/or they will be allowed to operate in an even more precarious state than they were in before.

3 Supply and Demand – in Practice

The relationship between the demand for some particular good and the amount of that good that will get supplied can be very complex. For example, short-term reactions to changes in either supply or demand can be very different to, or even the opposite of, long-term reactions. Economists typically use the mathematical tool *supply and demand curves* to model real-world economic behaviours. These curves are often required to slide up and down or left and right over time in order to accommodate awkward economic phenomena. Some economists have questioned the validity of using these curves as the basis of any economic analysis at all. In this chapter we will look at the idea of supply and demand without the use of those curves. This chapter is not intended to be comprehensive. It will only consider the types of market which will be useful to understand when developing arguments used later in the book.

The whole idea of supply and demand is that there are forces which drive them to be in equilibrium with each other. That is to say that if demand is greater than supply or supply is greater than demand then incentives will be created for actions to be taken which will tend to redress the balance. Table 3-1 shows the approximate nature of those actions.

Current state	True meaning	What will happen in the short term?	What will happen in the long term (perhaps several years)?
Demand greater than supply	The manufacturers can sell everything they make despite setting a price so high that they are more profitable than other comparable industries.	Manufacturers make large profits.	The company may be tempted to expand production. Potential rivals will observe the high profits to be made in this sector and be tempted to join in. Either action will eventually lead to more supply and lower prices.
Supply greater than demand	The only way that manufacturers can sell all that they make is to lower their prices to such a level that they are less profitable than other comparable industries.	Poor or even negative profits to be made.	Depending on the severity of the lack of demand, the companies may eventually start laying off staff, or go bust. Either of these actions will eventually lead to reduced supply and, so long as the market does not disappear altogether, higher prices.
Supply equals demand	Manufacturers are making profits on a par with comparable industries.	No change.	No change.

Table 3-1 Supply and demand.

Looking at this table, you may wonder why the actions described in the far right column are labelled as "long term". This is actually a bit of a generalisation and there are exceptions, but the gist is that the rate of production of a great many goods is rather awkward to change at short notice. In order to increase production, new machinery may need to be purchased, new factories built, new staff hired and trained. Depending on the industry this could take months or years. All of these things are very risky and companies may be reluctant to do them at all unless they are thoroughly convinced that the increase in demand is going to be sustained. They may well wish to monitor the demand for a while in order to build up the confidence to risk the money required for the new investment. Equally, decisions about reducing production may happen rather slowly. Business managers will usually be reluctant to make staff redundant for personal reasons. They may simply not give them any annual pay rise, or they may cut their pay. They may also be rather slow to make people redundant just in case the downturn in demand turns out to be temporary or the next marketing campaign saves the day.

This information contained in Table 3-1 can be converted into the more compact form of Table 3-2.

Balancing supply and demand for Product X can be restated as the combination of the following two phenomena, one that acts quickly and one that in general acts more slowly:		
The selling price of X is adjusted up or down such that the selling rate matches what producers can comfortably keep up with using existing factories, mines or workers.	+	If producers are making excess profits then consider increasing capacity.
		If producers are making insufficient profits then consider decreasing capacity.

Table 3-2 Simplified supply and demand.

As markets change and evolve, most of the time prices are tuned such that the selling rate approximately matches the *current* comfortable rate of production.

The model presented so far describes the supply and demand mechanism for a great deal, perhaps the majority, of normal goods and services. But there are a variety of special cases where things act a little differently. One such case is where the rate of supply of a good is not under the direct control of the people who sell it.

The special case of the supply not being in direct control of the producers

Imagine a company that sells bottled water from one particular spring. If the demand was to rise, there would be no way of creating any more supply. In this case the price would simply be adjusted upwards until the rate of sales again matched the rate of flow of the spring. This process simply corresponds to the left-hand side of Table 3-2 with the right-hand side unable to operate, i.e.:

In the special case of the supply not being in direct control of the producers, balancing supply and demand can be restated as simply:

Adjust the price such that you sell at a rate that matches what you can comfortably keep up with.

We shall be relying on this formulation later in the book in relation to bank lending.

Supply and demand for investment products

So far the discussions of supply and demand have all concerned goods which have a fairly straightforward and short path from production to sale and consumption. There are, however, some items of value that tend to change hands many times and are not so obviously "consumed"; for example, shares, bonds and houses.

The classical model of supply and demand now runs into a big problem which has not been fully appreciated by sections of the economics profession. For normal "consumed" goods it is usually obvious that higher prices deter buyers and low prices encourage buyers. Unfortunately too many economists believe that this principle applies equally to items purchased *as an investment or partially as an investment.*

To illustrate what is wrong with this idea, consider a hypothetical price history of Product X shown in Figure 3-1. Imagine that this is happening in a country with very low inflation, so the price rise is real. If Product X is a consumer good, perhaps a type of food, it is clear that the rising price will discourage purchases; people will increasingly consume some alternative foodstuff instead. But now imagine that X is an "investment product", something that people purchase in the hope that they can sell it on at a higher price at some later time. The classical laws of supply and demand would suggest that the current high price will deter purchases, but is it so clear that people will ignore the history of the price? How would you feel about purchasing this product as an investment? Would you ignore the history of the development of the price? How about a falling price history show in Figure 3-2. How would you feel about purchasing Product X with an eye to selling it on a few years later?

Figure 3-1 How a sustained history of rising prices makes an investment look good.

Figure 3-2 How a sustained history of falling prices makes an investment look bad.

The free market fundamentalists implicitly believe that virtually all investors completely ignore the history of the development of the price of investment products and base their purchasing decisions purely on the basis of the current price. In this book we take the view that many investors *do* indeed take the history of the current price into consideration as part of their decision to purchase or not. It is human nature to assume that almost anything that has been steadily behaving in a certain way for a long time will continue to behave in that way. This principle is built into the way our brains operate and learn. Mankind was confident that the sun would rise each morning *simply because it always had in the past*. This confidence came about long before any knowledge of gravity or the laws of motion. Everyone knows people who would insist that house prices would always go up, not because of any technical analysis of demographics and building regulations, but simply "because they always have". Keynes appeared to be well aware of this phenomenon when in 1937 he wrote:

> We assume that the present is a much more serviceable guide to the future than a candid examination of past experience would show it to have been hitherto. In other words we largely ignore the prospect of future changes about the actual character of which we know nothing.

For a detailed study of this kind of issue you could take a look at the book *Animal Spirits: How Human Psychology Drives the Economy and Why It Matters for Global Capitalism* by George Akerlof and Robert Shiller.

The act of taking the history of a price into consideration vandalises the simple law of supply and demand for that product. A high price can sometimes *entice* purchasing rather than discourage it, so long as the history of the price rise is perceived as steady rather than chaotic.

We shall consider the pricing of investment products in detail later in the book, but in preparation for that it will be useful to develop a simple way to visualise the behaviour of prices in response to patterns of buying and selling. Investment products, like shares and bonds, are often traded on some kind of exchange. The gist of the pricing mechanism is based on the fact that at any one time a small fraction of the market participants will be publicly advertising their intention to buy or sell. Often they will also be advertising the price they are willing to pay (or sell for). This collection of publicly visible "desires" can be monitored by the exchange and the information used to guide the price up or down by a (usually) small amount. The price is being continuously adjusted by the exchange so that the observed desire to buy equals the observed desire to sell. If some news came out that may cause the product to be more valuable, then there would be an increased desire to buy. The market would notice that there was suddenly an excess of people advertising their intention to buy and a dearth of people advertising their desire to sell. The price would then be adjusted upwards to encourage sellers and discourage buyers, until a new equilibrium was reached.

An approximate analogy can be made between this process and a physical model involving a bucket with two taps; see Figure 3-3. The tap at the top represents the flow of money from people keen to buy the commodity and the tap at the bottom represents the flow of money going to people keen to sell. The more money there is coming in from people keen to buy, the higher the price will go. The keener existing owners are to sell the commodity, the lower the price will go.

You will notice that the taps have been labelled "determined buying" and "determined selling". This is quite deliberate. We could not just label the taps "buying" and "selling" because for every buy there is a corresponding sell, and if it weren't for the fees charged for the transactions, the money coming in for buying would be exactly equal to the money going out as selling. What we have done instead is to define a "determined buy" as a trade where, at the last established price, the buyer is keener to buy than the seller is to sell and hence the buyer has to make a tempting offer of a price slightly above the previously established one in order for a seller to part with their commodity, hence establishing a new higher rate. Conversely a "determined sell" is a trade where the seller is keener to sell than the buyer is to buy, and hence the seller has to make a tempting offer of accepting a price slightly below the previously established one in order to persuade the buyer to buy the commodity, hence establishing a new lower going rate.

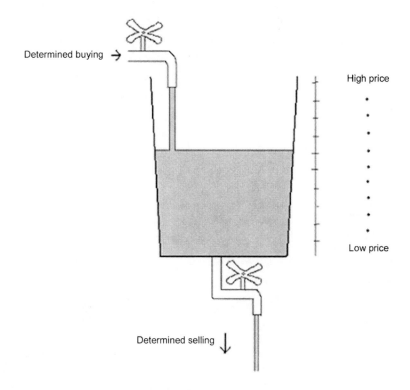

Figure 3-3 Visualisation of the price of traded products.

We shall be returning to expand on this model when analysing share prices in Chapter 13.

4 Savings and Unavoidable Ponzi Dynamics

Many economists treat money as if it were simply an intermediary in the exchange of goods and services, a store of value or something to replace the clumsy mechanism of barter. This book takes a different approach. It acknowledges that money itself can be a badly behaved, strange beast that can and does change its value or requires market-distorting government interventions to control. We will show how the use of money induces behaviours that simply would not occur in a barter world. In this book we shall consider economic phenomena, buying, selling, savings, loans etc., in these two steps:

1. Work out what the flow of goods and services would be without money.

2. Attempt to add in money, watching out for money being required to change its value in order for Step 1 to work.

Any behaviour that only occurs with the use of money, i.e. is absent in the world of barter, shall be deemed a *monetary phenomenon*. In doing this, we hope to show that monetary phenomena are a) very strong, b) affect almost every aspect of economics and c) if ignored, will lead economists and politicians to make some very bad decisions. We shall begin our journey with a closer look at savings.

The nature of savings

This chapter will consider the nature of savings, how their behaviour is rather different from what the textbooks would have you believe. In order to understand savings properly we need to clarify a few new terms and definitions which are different from how savings are normally discussed. First of all we will define three phases of the savings process: *set-up and prediction*, *monitoring* and *cashing in*. Then we shall consider the different types of savings: *simple warehouse, concentrated value* and *contract*. These definitions will help us consider the ways in which the value of your savings at the end of the process (when you come to "consume" them) can be much higher or lower than predicted at the start. We will show how savings are prone to something known as *Ponzi dynamics*. Finally we shall consider whether savings really have to be this way or whether the economy could be configured to be more stable and predictable.

Storing value?

People rarely stop to think about what is really happening when we save. We just assume that we're "storing value", metaphorically as if we had a big warehouse of goods that we put things in ready to be consumed at a later date. There are many misconceptions about savings that we need to address in order to have a better understanding of economics. But in order to appreciate these misconceptions we need to be a little pedantic for a moment and consider precisely what savings *really* are.

Say that you are fit, well and productive right now and could, if you wanted, live comfortably enough **consuming less than you produce**. You may want to somehow use this spare capacity to arrange that in the future you can get by in a situation where you are **producing less than you consume**. There are many possible reasons for this desire:

- saving for your retirement

- saving so that you can support yourself during some period of retraining for a new career

- saving just in case something bad happens, like losing your job and having to survive through a temporary period of unemployment.

We can now state that:

> **Savings are the mechanism by which you attempt to translate a period of producing more than you consume during one part in your life into a supply of goods and services at a later time.**

The word "attempt" in the definition is quite deliberate and must not be left out because there are a multitude of things that can go wrong in the process, some obvious and some rather subtle and deceptive.

In many economics textbooks savings and investments are treated quite differently. Savings are described as a kind of passive, non-speculative activity in which you simply "store" value. Investments, however, are seen as a more exciting activity in which you aim to get out more than you put in; you carefully select some business project to invest in. If the business succeeds you may multiply your investment. If the business fails you may lose everything.

Clearly savings and investments have some different characteristics, but you may notice the definition of savings just given in this book encapsulates both. Indeed the boundary between savings and

43

investments is often blurred. For example, when you go and put your money in a "savings account", you may feel that you are just "saving". You are supposedly taking no risk. There is no chance of losing your savings, and similarly no chance that you will hit the jackpot and suddenly have your savings shoot up in value. But now just consider what happens with that money. The bank may very well take your "savings" and use it to invest in companies on the stock exchange. You think you are saving via a middleman, but that middleman promptly turns round and uses your money for investing! In this chapter we will take the unusual step of considering saving and investments together and labelling both as simply different flavours of "saving".

There is a general feeling, certainly among the public, that when you save you almost invariably get out more than you put in, or at the very worst, about the same as what you put in. The only way you can lose out is if you speculated on something risky. You chose the wrong thing. You were the fool that made a mistake while the bulk of everyone else did better. The possibility that the *bulk* of a population's savings could fail all at once is scarcely considered as something within the realms of possibility. Most economics textbooks will gloss over this possibility in their discussions of savings. Mass savings failures seem to be a kind of specialist subject, only to be considered by a small percentage of professional economists that make a special study of those intermittent economic catastrophes. The bulk of economics students will graduate with the impression that savings are a reliable thing.

Some books describe savings in terms of preferences... you may "prefer" to consume your stuff now or may prefer to consume at a later date. It seems almost as if you are in a shop choosing which kind of cake you want. There is little clue in the language used that you may in fact be choosing between one kind of cake and a 50% chance of getting the other kind.

In this chapter we hope to show that there is no such thing as a safe type of savings. All savings have the potential to fail to some degree or other, even ones that get erroneously defined as 100% safe in the textbooks, like government bonds.

Before we can go on to discuss these failure mechanisms we need to establish some more concepts and terminology. First of all we need to consider the different stages of the savings process and then the different types of saving mechanism.

There are many types of savings, but whichever one is used we can identify three stages in the process:

1. **Set up and prediction.** The "set up" part is the point at which savings are instigated. We put money in the bank, we buy some bonds, we invest in some shares etc. The "prediction" is our estimate of what we will be able to get in terms of goods and services at that future point in time where we intend to "consume" our savings. Our enthusiasm for saving and our decisions about how much to save may be influenced by our prediction.

2. **Monitoring.** Very often it will be possible to monitor the progress of the value of our savings. These rises and falls may influence our decisions about whether or not to make more or less *additional* savings.

3. **Consumption or cashing in.** This is that point at a future time when we decide to, or need to, consume more than we produce. We now need to convert or "cash in" some or all of our savings to translate into goods and services.

So now we are ready introduce the different types of saving and for each one we will consider its practicality, predictability and stability.

Savings type 1: Simple warehouse

The crudest form of saving, we will call *simple warehouse*. This is where you quite literally build up a store of the things you will need in case of a rainy day. For this type of savings you will need storage space. If you need to save for a sustained period, the space will need to be quite large, perhaps a warehouse. You will have to either rent or buy this warehouse and maintain it. You may also need to hire a security guard to make sure nothing gets stolen. All the food you store will have to be tinned or frozen. If it's frozen you will have to pay for the electricity to run the freezer. If you store things over a very long period you may find that some items gradually become redundant. That collection of floppy discs and VHS cassettes and that record player may all be pretty useless by the time you reach a point when you need to get by on, or consume, your savings. Finally you will notice that services, like medical care or hairdressing, cannot be saved via this mechanism at all.

At this point you will hopefully be getting the idea that the warehouse savings method is riddled with problems and nobody in their right minds would even attempt to save in this way over a sustained period in our modern society. We can summarise this as follows:

> **Warehouse savings are highly problematic and don't work for services at all.**

Needless to say this savings mechanism is scarcely used in the real world today.

Savings type 2: Concentrated value storage

Anyone looking at a description of the simple warehouse mechanism may be thinking to themselves, "Don't be silly – you shouldn't attempt to save the *full range* of things that you use every day!" The obvious fix to this stupidity is the following: When you want to save, trade in your produce for something that has high value in a compact and durable form, perhaps gold or diamonds. This can be stored far more cheaply. At a later time, when you need to live off your savings, you just trade your gold/diamonds back into the full spectrum of goods and services you need. We will label this mechanism *concentrated value storage*.

At first glance this mechanism appears to solve just about all the problems associated with the simple warehouse method. The costs of storage will be relatively low and you can have complete flexibility as to exactly what goods you can get in the future as well as the option to get services.

This type of savings appears to be very safe and pedestrian. Surely there is no risk involved, is there? Surely we just get out the same as we put in and there's nothing else to it. Unfortunately not. This type of savings can perform well or badly for reasons rarely discussed in the textbooks. We shall illustrate how with a series of three thought experiments. In the first experiment we will present a simple scenario in which the savings perform well. Then, as we add more realism, we will begin to see instability creep in.

Thought experiment 1: Very few people saving

Let us imagine an island where there are only two types of good, namely potatoes and jewels. These choices are actually surrogates for essential, perishable goods and non-essential, non-perishable goods. There is no money, no banks, only barter. The potatoes grow year round and in living memory the harvests have never failed. For the sake of simplicity, let's assume that all the jewels in the world are of similar size and quality, as are potatoes. Let's also state that all the jewels in the land that could ever be found have already been found. There are no more mines or other sources, so the total quantity of jewels is fixed.

Some islanders like to have jewels to wear and show off their status at social events. Jewels are relatively rare and so when trading they may command an exchange rate of, say, 100 potatoes each. Everyone on this island has ample land and they make their own huts from the plentiful wood and leaves. There is very little demand for any savings on this island because old people get looked after by their children so there is no need to save up in any way for old age. In this scenario we would expect the exchange rate between jewels and potatoes to be dominated by their scarcity and value purely as fashion items.

In this scenario imagine that you are a bit of a worrier; perhaps you have no family and few friends and are worried that you may get ill at some point and not have the energy to forage for potatoes. Having some savings will help you get through that potential hard time ahead. Imagine also that very few others have such concerns, so few others simultaneously want to save. In order to "save", you would now trade some of your excess potatoes for jewels at the going rate. Let's say this is around 100 to 1. Then at a future time, when you needed to live off your savings, you could trade in your jewels for potatoes at approximately the same rate. Your savings have been 100% efficient.

To summarise:

> **In a scenario where very few people save, the value of jewels will be predominantly a function of their desirability as fashion accessories. Any rare person who does choose to use jewels as a "savings conduit" will find their savings to be perfectly efficient.**

Thought experiment 2: Lots of people saving (steady state assumption)

In this variation, you are not the only one wanting to save. Lots of people want to save for the future for one reason or another. Perhaps it is not the tradition for the elderly to be looked after by their children. Under these conditions there would be a strong desire for retirement savings. Jewels would now generally be seen as dual purpose, both a fashion item and a "savings conduit".

So now let's consider what the exchange rate between jewels and potatoes might be compared to the case where very few people saved. In the world without much savings, consider the pool of people who may be tempted to buy jewels. Clearly not everyone has that desire equally. Jewels are non-essential, a matter of taste. Some people may have no interest in them at all while others may crave them. Among the population there will be a certain distribution of desire for jewels. This is shown as a Venn diagram in Figure 4-1.

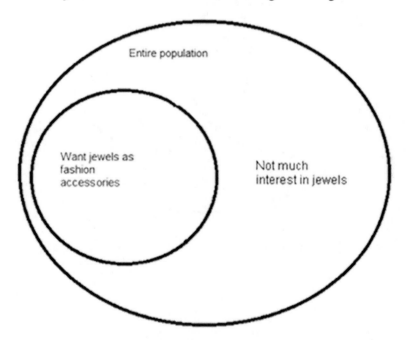

Entire population

Want jewels as fashion accessories

Not much interest in jewels

Figure 4-1 The desire for jewels when there is no need for savings.

Now consider a situation in which there is a great desire for savings and jewels are now dual purpose. The desire for jewels as a fashion item will not have diminished, but now there will be a new, additional distribution of desires for jewels as a savings conduit. There will be some people who had no desire for jewels as a fashion accessory but do have a desire for jewels for savings. This new combined collection of desires will be greater than the original and the price will be higher, i.e. the exchange rate with potatoes will be raised. Let's say that it could be perhaps 200 potatoes per jewel. This new desire for jewels is illustrated in Figure 4-2.

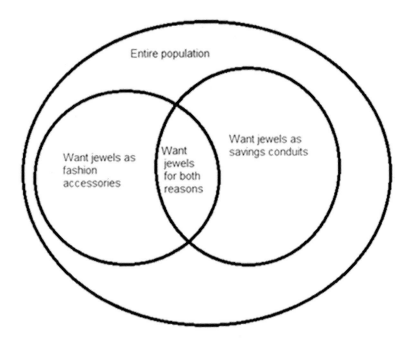

Figure 4-2 Desire for jewels when also used for savings.

In this thought experiment we are assuming, perhaps unrealistically, that the rate of new people starting to save is in constant balance with the rate of previous savers now starting to live off their savings. The potato/jewel exchange rate will be steady.

It should be noted that under these circumstances it is easy for savers to predict the final value of their savings and their savings will all be efficient. People will get out pretty much the same as what they put in.

To summarise:

> **In a scenario where there is a large but stable desire for saving, the value of jewels will be partly a function of their desirability as fashion accessories and partly a function of their desirability as savings conduits. Anyone who uses jewels as a "savings conduit" will find their savings to be perfectly efficient and predictable.**

Thought experiment 3: Lots of people saving (more realistic assumptions)

So far the thought experiments have resulted in scenarios where savings are very well behaved, predictable and efficient. This is all about to change.

Let's consider what happens if the desire for savings within the society is not constant. This could occur for a wide variety of reasons in the real world:

- demographics, e.g. immigration, emigration, lifespan changes, changes in the average number of children per family

- tax changes

- regulatory changes

- changes in social norms, e.g. changes in the propensity for children to look after their parents in old age

- optimism/pessimism about future wealth / job security.

It is important to note that there is a wide variety of timescales over which these changes can occur. Some, like regulatory changes, may happen overnight, while others, like changes to the average number of children per family, may play out over decades.

The result of any of these changes is that the balance between new people wanting to start saving and previous savers wanting to start living off their savings, will no longer be steady and subsequently the exchange rate between jewels and potatoes will no longer be steady. We can approximately sum up the expected jewel/potato exchange rate in the following table:

New people wanting to save greater than existing savers wanting to cash in	Upward pressure on the price of jewels
Existing savers wanting to cash in greater than new people wanting to start saving	Downward pressure on the price of jewels

Table 4-1 Factors affecting the price of jewels.

Changes in the jewel/potato exchange rate over time are illustrated in Figure 4-3.

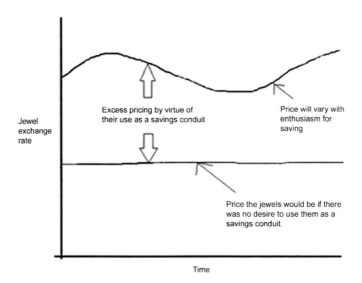

Figure 4-3 How variability in desire for savings affects jewel price.

If in general there was little need for savings, i.e. the circle on the right-hand side of the Venn diagram in Figure 4-2 was far smaller than the one on the left, then the price of jewels would be dominated by their desirability as fashion accessories. The area of the circle on the right could double or halve without having much effect on the selling price. If, however, things were the other way round, i.e. the circle on the right was far larger than the one on the left, then the price of jewels would be dominated by the demand for savings. Now that same doubling or halving of the desire for savings would have an enormous effect on the price of jewels. We can sum up the situation as follows:

> **The greater the need for savings in society, the more variable the price of commodities used as savings conduits will be.**

A generally high demand for savings by society as a whole makes it much harder to predict how much you will get out at the other end when you start saving.

Let's now consider who is buying and selling the jewels at any one time and their motivations:

	Buyers (people whose actions push the price up)	**Sellers** (people whose actions push the price down)
Relatively stable part	**Group A:** People wanting to buy jewels predominantly as fashion items	**Group B:** People who had previously owned jewels as fashion items deciding they want to sell
Unstable part	**Group C:** New savers wanting to buy jewels as savings conduits	**Group D:** Ex-savers wanting to cash in

Table 4-2 Factors affecting the price of jewels – more detail.

If Groups C and D are large and dominate jewel trading then the price can said to be being "kept up" by C. The value that Group D can get when they cash in, will be predominantly determined by the process of selling their jewels to Group C. If C shrank relative to D, then the price would fall.

This mechanism can now be seen to have what has been referred to as *Ponzi dynamics.*

Charles Ponzi 1882–1949

Charles Ponzi was an Italian swindler. The gist of his scam was an "investment scheme". People would invest their money in return for a very high rate of return. Little did the investors know that the money they were able to take out from the scheme was made up mostly from the money of new investors joining the scheme rather than from any skilful investing. This could only continue so long as there was an ever-increasing supply of new investors. Clearly this state could not continue indefinitely, and sure enough in 1920 the scheme collapsed and Charles Ponzi was sent to prison.

Bernard Madoff operated a scam on the same basis and was caught out in 2008.

Normally people consider Ponzi schemes as something illegal, occasionally attempted by a rogue criminal. But Ponzi dynamics in savings cannot be avoided; they are "baked in". They are a natural consequence of the variability of savings desires.

So we now see that the efficiency of savings will vary depending on the balance between ex-savers cashing-in and new savers starting to save. This appears to be a nuisance, an irritation, an effect that leads to variations in savings efficiency that we hope is not too large. Sadly, there is worse to come. There are feedback mechanisms at play. The problem is that the changes in the jewel exchange rate brought about by changes in the balance between new savers and ex-savers, in and of itself, serves to affect the imbalance. In order to explore the nature of the feedback, let's imagine for minute that the price of the jewels had been rising steadily for a sustained period, for some reason. Consider the reaction to this scenario by some different groups within society:

Group	Reaction to sustained rise in price of savings conduit
"I currently have few or no savings but it is essential that I start to save for my pension. I need X amount of goods and services in my old age."	"Savings values appear to grow so well that I only need put away a small amount for the future." This person may be fooled into putting in too little for their pension.
"It is optional that I save in the short to medium term. I may be tempted to save if my prediction of the cash-in value is substantially more then what I put in. I may attempt to use this growth in savings value as a form of ongoing income."	Encouraged to save.
"I already have some savings. I am in stage 2 of the savings process: the monitoring phase."	"Wow, my savings are doing so well. I'm going to be very comfortable in my old age. I certainly don't need to add to my savings. Indeed I could even cash in some of my savings early, consume them and *still* have enough for the future."

Table 4-3 Reaction to sustained price changes.

It is hard to say exactly which way this feedback will end up, positive or negative, because the rising price of jewels will affect different groups in different ways. Also, at any one time there may be different proportions of people in the different situations, some encouraged to save more, others encouraged to save less. One thing you can say for certain is that if people are unaware of the Ponzi dynamics at play and they assume that the price changes are based on purely non-Ponzi reasons, then they are liable to make mistakes in both the prediction and monitoring phases of their savings plans. This will cause there to be periods in which there is a tendency for people save more than they otherwise would and other periods where people will save less than they otherwise would.

Sadly when you go and see a pensions advisor to ask how much you need to put aside each month in order to have a decent pension, it is unlikely they will warn you of Ponzi dynamics at play.

Savings type 3: Contract savings

So now we come on to the next form of savings which we will call *contract saving*. This is where you find someone who is keen to get hold of your excess production now in return for an agreement that they will "repay" you with goods or services at some point in the future. There is no need for the goods used for repayment to even be in existence at the time that the agreement is made.

The wording of the contract can take a very wide variety of forms, for example:

> **"I'll give you one fridge, a Hoover and a washing machine in return for you giving me a television, an iPod and a games console at some time in the future."**

or

> **"I'll give you one month's worth of whatever I produce in my workplace now, then you give me one month's worth of whatever you produce in your workplace at some time in the future."**

But the real advantage over warehouse and concentrated value savings can be seen in the following example contract:

"I'll give you a collection of goods and services now to enable you to build a new factory and start a business. If the business is profitable then at some time in the future you give me a collection of goods and services taken from the profits of that company. I expect this to be much larger than the collection I gave you in the first place to compensate me for the risk that the business will fail."

This specific form of contract could be labelled an *investment contract*. It is this form of contract that lies at the heart of capitalism. Out of all the savings mechanisms seen so far, this one appears to have hit the jackpot. Not only can we translate our superfluous goods and services now into the future, but we have a mechanism for getting more in the future than we put in. Not that this can't happen with concentrated value savings, but with this form of contract savings we can see an explicit mechanism for growing the value of our savings conduit.

A real-world example of this kind of contract would be purchasing an original share in a company, holding on to the share and collecting dividend payments.

Note that purchasing shares on the secondary market was not used as an example, for reasons that will be discussed later.

Definitions:	
Shares	Documents declaring part ownership of a company.
Dividends	The mechanism by which company profits are distributed among its owners.
Secondary market	When a company initially sells some of its shares, Person X may purchase some of them. X's money will go to the company. If Person X then sells on their shares in the secondary market, Person Y may purchase them. Y's money will go to X, not the company.

Table 4-4 Some share-related definitions.

Contract savings need a willing partner

There is a fundamental difference between contract savings and either simple warehouse or concentrated value savings. Contract savings need a willing party on the other side of the deal. The person on the other side of the contract must have a desire to do the opposite of saving. They must be keen to borrow. *Borrowing* is the consumption of goods and services now in return for an obligation to pay back goods and services in the future. In a steady state equilibrium there would be equal enthusiasm for borrowing and saving. Everyone keen to do some saving would be able to find a corresponding person keen to do some borrowing. But as we have already seen, there are many reasons for saving/borrowing enthusiasm to get out of balance. When the balance is unequal then one side will be able to drive a harder bargain. This can be summed up in the following table:

Bias	Typical deal struck
Excess of savers over borrowers	"I'll give you a large amount of goods and services now in return for a small amount of goods and services in the future."
Excess of borrowers over savers	"I'll give you a small amount of goods and services now in return for a large amount of goods and services in the future."

Table 4-5 Effects of unequal desires for saving and borrowing.

Money acts as a form of contract savings

If your job is to make a product or offer a service then when you exchange your good or service for money, the dollar bills are a kind of contract with the rest of society. The dollar bills could be considered to be a contract saying: "In return for those goods or services you just gave to one particular individual within our society, we will give you some goods or services of your choice at a time in the future of your choosing to be collected from *any* member of society."

To make this clearer, we can illustrate this with the following two diagrams. First of all there is the savings set-up stage, where you may exchange your goods or services that you produce to Man A, who of course is part of society, in return for a contract, i.e. dollar bills, promising goods or services in the future.

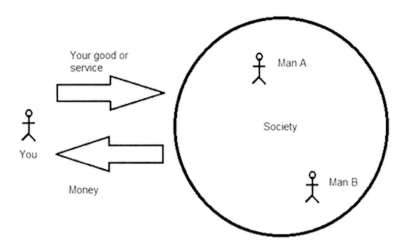

Figure 4-4 Selling your produce "to society".

Now at a later time we arrive at the consumption phase of the savings process. We can consume our savings by swapping the contract, i.e. some dollar bills, for a collection of goods or services to be delivered by Man B, another member of society.

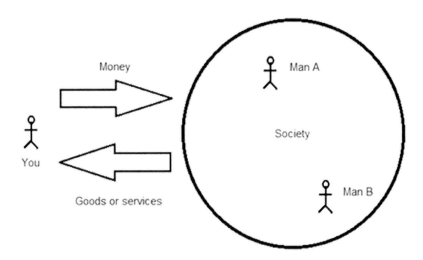

Figure 4-5 Purchasing goods "from society".

It's almost as if society is a large company where the management has given every "employee" the authority to arrange contracts with you.

Money on its own, i.e. simply "stored under the mattress", is normally a rather poor form of savings because governments, in conjunction with the banking system, usually conspire to create ever increasing amounts of it, thereby reducing the amount of goods and services that can be purchased at the consumption stage.

The stability and predictability of contract savings

We have already seen how concentrated value savings can suffer from swings in value due to Ponzi dynamics. In this section we will consider how contract savings compare.

The predictability of contract savings depends very much on the wording of the contract. We shall now consider the characteristics of a variety of forms.

Short name: "DAYS' WORK SWAP"

Contract type: "I'll give you X days' worth of my goods and services now in return for Y days' worth of whatever you produce in the future."

Predictability: This simple-sounding arrangement is actually highly predictable for long-term savings. If your plan is to be able to support yourself for a period of length Y in the future, then it is very easy to know how much of this type of arrangement to make.

What could go wrong? The person on the other side of this deal may die or become incapacitated. This risk can be mitigated by making multiple smaller-scale arrangements with a number of different people.

Popularity: Despite the good stability and predictability of this arrangement, not many contracts of this type are drawn up in the real world today.

Short name: "MONEY SWAP"

Contract type: "I'll give you \$X now, so that you can buy some goods or services, in return for \$Y in the future."

Predictability: This type of contract is hard to predict over extended periods in terms of what collection of goods and services could be purchased with \$Y. If there is an unexpected, sustained period of high inflation then the value of the savings at the consumption stage could be decimated. Conversely if the set-up stage for this contract was made during a period of high inflation then the person on the other end of the contract may set their value of Y accordingly high. If inflation then unexpectedly drops or even becomes negative (it can happen) then that person may struggle to be able to get \$Y together at the end of the contract and may be forced to default.

What could go wrong? Unexpected changes in the rate of inflation, either up or down.

Popularity: Despite the many problems with predictability and the risk of default, this is a very popular form of contract in the real world today.

Short name: "INVESTMENT FOR PROFITS SWAP"

Contract type: "I'll give you $X now so that you can start a business, in return for Y% of the profits of that business in the future."

Example: This type of contract corresponds to buying some original shares in a business, then holding on to them and collecting the dividend payments.

Predictability: While there may be great variability in the value that can be extracted, a skilled investor should be able to arrange a bias toward getting more out than was put in. The variability of this form of contract can be reduced markedly by making multiple smaller contracts with a wide variety of businesses. The predictability of this type of contract is essentially one and the same thing as your skill in predicting the profitability of new companies.

What could go wrong? If you are a poor judge of the future profitability of new companies then your savings may lose value.

Popularity: This is done to some degree in the real world today, though it is not nearly as often practised as an alternative, more complicated variation which we come to next.

Short name: "VALUE CHANGE SEQUENCE"

Contract type: A multi-step chain of contracts as follows…

"I'll give you $A now, for that certificate of ownership of part of that existing business X, which I will then sell a short time later for $B" – followed by…

"I'll give you $B now, for that certificate of ownership of part of that existing business Y, which I will then sell a short time later for $C" – followed by…

"I'll give you $C now, for that certificate of ownership of part of that existing business Z, which I will then sell a short time later for $D"

etc. etc.

Example: This corresponds to buying and selling shares on a frequent basis, making money predominantly from changes in the price of the shares rather than from dividend payments.

Predictability: Many economists appear to assume that the value change sequence method of savings is simply a more flexible form of the investment for profits swap. They assume that all the characteristics with regard to stability and predictability are identical. This assumption could not be more untrue. Unfortunately the precise reasons this assumption is false is complicated, but they will be explained in detail later in the book.

What could go wrong? Many things. We shall discuss these later in the book.

Popularity: This form of savings is enormously popular. The pensions provisions of millions of people are dependent on this mechanism.

As you can see, the popularity of different contract savings mechanisms is rather at odds with their inherent predictability and stability. If we want to design a more stable economic system then this contradiction will need to be addressed.

Saving scenario thought experiments

So now we have considered some properties of the savings process. It will be useful to work through some specific scenarios.

A model of the introduction of pensions

Coming back to the jewel and potato world, let's say that the society starts out in a state where there is little desire for savings. Traditionally the children look after their parents when they eventually become too old and frail to get food for themselves. This has been the status quo for many generations. Then there is a change in society. For some reason there is a move toward the idea of people *saving* toward their old age. People are now encouraged to buy jewels as a savings conduit through their working lives so that when they become elderly they can cash in their jewels to get by.

In the early years of this transition, the price of jewels will rise as more and more are purchased as a savings conduit. Note that in this phase there will be very few old people in the cashing-in stage, i.e. there will be very few ex-savers in the process of selling jewels to get by. The savers will be monitoring the progress of the value of the savings in order to judge just how many jewels they will need to buy in their working years. They will observe unusually high and rising prices of jewels. This will naturally lead people to believing that they don't need to collect many jewels in order to get by. If people are unaware of Ponzi dynamics at play then the high and rising prices may erroneously be attributed to spurious other factors.

A few decades may pass in this "optimistic" state, but then things will start to change. There will be a gradual rise in the number of people becoming old and entering the stage where they need to sell their jewels. More people selling will naturally lead to a lower price. People entering their latter years will now be disappointed to see that the previous estimated value of their savings conduits was too optimistic. There may be too little time left to correct the error and their final years may be spent in poverty. Figure 4-6 illustrates the evolution of the price of jewels in the process.

It is important to realise that should the new "saving for your old age idea" remain in place for generations to come, with a constant population, the jewel price would eventually stabilise at a new level and the number of savings errors would eventually reduce. It is large *changes* in savings propensity that lead to the errors.

Another feature that may have stood a chance of reducing this type of saving error is simply to ensure that the economics textbooks were teaching students to pay attention to the Ponzi dynamics inherent in most savings mechanisms.

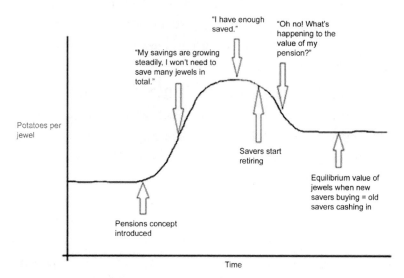

Figure 4-6 The introduction of pensions.

One criticism of this explanation may be to say that with such a simple scenario it may be obvious to everyone what is happening. The participants would never be so stupid. Indeed in the jewel and potato world this may be the case. In the real world however, we have many additional complicating factors like the use of money, fractional reserve banking, international trade and many others. These factors all serve to obfuscate the fundamentals of what is going on under the surface. They also mean that when Ponzi dynamics drive up the price of a commodity, it is virtually certain that there will be *other* things that economists can point to as explanations. Indeed there can be multiple reasons for price changes all going on at the same time. When this is the case, Ponzi dynamics are usually the last thing on the minds of economists.

A demonstration of how one person saving can work but everyone saving can fail

It is an inherent feature of savings mechanisms that the number of people simultaneously attempting to save can have an impact on the success of those savings. We shall illustrate this with another thought experiment.

Imagine that it has been arranged that 10,000 *sterile* people (sterile in the sense that, they can not reproduce), who are all 20 years old, are placed on an island that is separated from the rest of the world. Each one is given a sum of money to trade with. When they get to the island each person specialises in making whatever it is that they have the skills to make and they all trade with each other using the money that they were given. Now imagine a particular islander, let's call him Tom. One day he has a thought: he realises that when he becomes elderly he's going to be weaker and slow down. He won't be able to make so much stuff that he can trade for food etc. So he decides to save a certain fraction of his money under the mattress for his old age. Let's also imagine that Tom is the only person who had this realisation and he didn't tell anyone else.

Now fast forward a few decades... Tom is now 80 years old, as are all the other islanders. Tom is now in a much better state than the rest of the population. He can use his saved money to buy extra stuff to make sure he can keep his standard of living just as high as it was when he was younger.

Now let's consider what would happen if everyone was saving...

In this scenario Tom has the same realisation about his old age, but this time he tells everyone else. This time *everyone* on the island decides to save for their old age. They're all worried that when they slow down they won't be able to keep up their standard of living unless they save. Now you can imagine what's coming...

Fast forward a few decades and now everyone is 80 years old. Everyone has slowed down and is producing less stuff per day. It is easy to see that on average everyone's standard of living will go down in old age in exactly the same way as if they hadn't bothered to save at all. Everyone *thought* they were saving to prop up their future lifestyles – but they were deluding themselves.

Notice that there is the same amount of money throughout the experiment. So when the now elderly population are producing a smaller quantity of goods and services with an unchanged quantity of money in the system, the average cost of those goods will naturally rise. Notice that *the purchasing power (value) of money changes in order that an undeniable truth is enforced.*

Conclusion

Hopefully at this point you can see that the entire concept of savings is far more unstable than may appear at first glance. The value of savings conduits can go up and down en masse, and this variability can in and of itself cause feedbacks which have the potential to induce further variability, turning some minor variations into larger swings. This variability will inevitably lead to errors in the prediction and or monitoring phases of the savings process.

Prediction errors in savings can have devastating effects. People who had been putting too little away for their retirements for decades because they had been deluded into thinking that their pension pots were growing strongly may unexpectedly find that they have to spend the last years of their lives in poverty. And sadly this is not the end of the story with regard to the instability of savings. In later chapters we shall see how the behaviour of fractional reserve banking can further interfere with the savings process to make the instability and feedback problems even worse.

5 Inflation Misconceptions

Everyone knows what inflation is, don't they? We see prices of goods going up in the shops year after year; that's inflation, isn't it?...

Inflation is usually defined in mainstream economics textbooks as something like "a rise in the general level of prices of goods and services in an economy over a period of time". At first glance this seems quite straightforward – surely economists must fully understand everything there is to know about inflation? Sadly there are a variety of factors that make inflation an altogether more complicated phenomenon.

In this chapter we shall look into inflation in a little more detail, just enough to help you understand some inflation-related mistakes that economists, politicians and central bankers have been making for years.

Rise in the prices of what?

Okay, so inflation is some kind of rise in prices but it is critical to ask, "Rise in the prices of what?" The textbook answer is "goods and services" which, many people have an approximate notion, means kind of, well, "everything", or "everything that can be purchased by anyone". This is where problems arise. The standard measures of inflation used by governments and economists, for example the Consumer Price Index (CPI), or Retail Price Index (RPI) in the UK, are generally measures of the price of goods and services that *householders* buy. At this point you may be thinking, well, that's "everything", isn't it? Unfortunately not. "Goods and services that householders buy" falls well short of "everything". There are all sorts of things that can be purchased in an economy by people other than householders; for example, company stocks, bonds and financial derivatives that are purchased by bankers. The price of them is not included in the normal inflation measures in any way.

Now you could argue that it is not really essential to measure the cost of *everything* to get an estimate of inflation so long as, broadly speaking, there is a tendency for prices of different types of good to rise in step with each other. Just from your own experiences you probably get the feeling that the price of goods tend to, broadly speaking, be in step. Now this may be true if the goods are related, like, say, different kinds of food. But when looking at very different items, the price changes can be extremely different. Goods that can be made more efficiently with technological advances often decrease in price as other goods rise. The price of computers and home music systems is an example of that. By contrast the price of items for which technology will make little difference will be far more resistant to falls. The price of a one-hour back massage will probably never be reduced due to any technological progress.

The cost of living

The reason that inflation measures, as used by governments, measure the kinds of things that householders spend their money on is tied to the fact the governments need a measure of changes to the *cost of living*, i.e. a measure of changes in how much money is required for people to get by on. This is useful for determining changes to things like wages for government workers and social security benefits. These kinds of payments are very often *index linked*, that is to say their value will go up in proportion to the CPI or RPI. This makes perfect sense; if the cost of living goes up by 5% then governments should pay 5% more as unemployment benefit. It is because of this usefulness that governments will go to the trouble of employing all the people required to collate the CPI/RPI data. These measures will be widely published and well known by economists, politicians and the general public. For the sake of clarity we shall in future refer to these measures as *cost of living inflation*.

Cost of living inflation is a political issue

The public have a notion of inflation; they think of inflation as rises in the prices of the kinds of things they have to pay for or buy on a regular basis, and because of this governments pay lots of attention to it. In recent history cost of living inflation has been a real problem in many countries, often in the second or third worlds but occasionally in the first world too. During 1975 the cost of living inflation reached 24.2% in the UK and in 1980 it was just short of 15% in the US. Any government presiding over a period of high cost of living inflation will be ridiculed mercilessly by the political opposition.

Another reason that cost of living inflation is a political issue is that people can see it with their own eyes. There is little a government can do to hide it. People know when the price of goods goes up in the shops. It may become the subject of dinner table conversations and newspaper articles. People will always grumble about rises in the cost of living, even if their wages go up correspondingly!

People observing big price rises will be disinclined to re-elect the incumbent governments so politicians are always keen to be able to announce that the latest inflation figures are low.

The price of houses is not included!

So cost of living inflation attempts to measure changes in the price of the things that ordinary householders buy, but when it comes to housing we have a dilemma: how do we measure the cost of housing? Is the cost of housing the size of the mortgage repayments or the actual purchase price of the house? It could perhaps be argued either way but the way that most governments have ended up choosing, is to measure the cost of the mortgage repayments. This may make sense from the point of view of measuring exactly what people have to pay on a regular basis, but it does mean that the actual purchase price of houses is hidden from the inflation measures: If interest rates drifted downwards to some unusually low level while at the same time house prices drifted upwards, then it would be possible for mortgage repayments to remain constant. The CPI measure would report "no inflation going on here!" while the price of the largest items the public ever purchase was steadily rising.

Relation to the amount of money

It has become a consensus that the main cause of long-term inflation is the gradual increase in the total amount of money in the economy (the money supply), though the way that this gets discussed in economics textbooks is often too crude. For example it is often stated that "if governments print too much money then this leads to inflation". This is based on the misguided assumption that the money supply is simply a fixed multiple of the monetary base. Unfortunately, as we have already seen, the relationship between the *monetary base* (the money governments create directly) and the *money supply* (the much larger amount of money created by the banks, in the lending and re-lending process) is very far from fixed. The money supply is determined far more by people's propensity to take out new loans versus people's propensity to pay back (or default on) existing loans.

The relationship between the size of the monetary base and the money supply has weakened in recent decades as the size of the monetary base as a fraction of the total money supply has shrunk dramatically. This fact does not seem to be appreciated by the vast majority of economists. To illustrate the point, take a look at Figure 5-1 which shows the year-on-year change in the amount of money the Unites States government "prints", i.e. changes to the monetary base", and the year-on-year change in the CPI. The correspondence between the two curves is clearly poor.

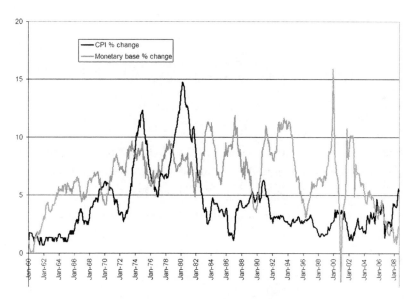

Figure 5-1 CPI changes v. monetary base changes.

You may notice that the graph ends just before the crash of 2008. The reason for that is that the change in the monetary base at the end of 2008 was so astounding that it requires the graph to be re-drawn on a different scale altogether; see Figure 5-2. As you can see the monetary base increased over 100% (from around $800 billion to $1.8 trillion) in one year, and just look at the CPI inflation in the same period: It was negative!

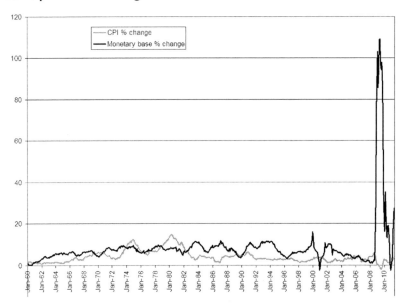

Figure 5-2 CPI v. monetary base – zoomed out.

At this point you may be thinking, "Okay, so changes to the monetary base don't correlate very well, or even at all with CPI inflation, but presumably the actual money supply will." Take a look at Figure 5-3. Again it is very hard to discern any correlation. Indeed you could even argue that there is perhaps a slight inverse correlation. There seem to be many places where peaks in one curve coincide with dips in the other.

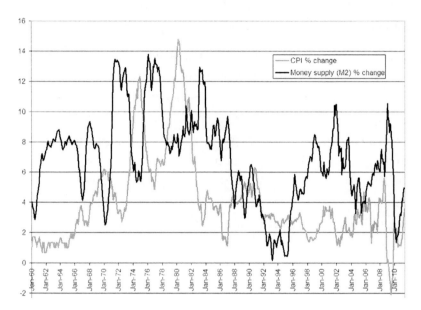

Figure 5-3 CPI changes v. money supply changes.

This result seems counterintuitive: Surely if the amount of money in the economy goes up, then for a given level of trade prices must go up too. Or to put it another way: Imagine that overnight all the dollars (real or electronic) were multiplied by ten, then surely shopkeepers would quickly catch on and put their prices up by a factor of ten too. So how is it even possible that prices don't rise and fall in step with the money supply? Surely the supply and demand mechanism would see to that? The answer is that eventually they probably do but there is a complication: It's the average price of *everything* that goes up and down with the money supply not just household purchases, and as we shall see later, an increase in the money supply does not cause an equal rise in the price of consumer goods versus the price of financial instruments that banks buy, like company shares.

Rises in the price of shares are often (incorrectly) applauded

Increases in the price of shares are not included in most government measures of inflation. Inflation is seen by most people as a bad thing, whereas rises in the price shares is seen by most as unquestionably good, the sign of a flourishing economy. Why should this be so? Nobody would ever say that about electronic goods. Can you imagine a politician gleefully announcing that the price of flat-screen televisions was steadily rising, or had reached an all time high? The reason for this difference in attitude is that shares are considered an investment. And presumably rises in the price of investments can only be a good thing for an economy, and so rising share prices surely couldn't have anything to do with that nasty inflation phenomenon, could they? In this section we will argue that they most certainly do.

A short digression on the price of stocks

Stocks are a share, or part ownership of a company. When companies make a profit, they may choose to pay out part or all of it to the shareholders. The sharing out of profits is called *dividend payments*. **Dividends are essentially the only reason shares have any value at all.** You may have noticed that some people buy shares for a short period in the hope that they will rise in price and they will be perfectly happy to sell them on without having collected any dividend payments, so long as they can sell them for more than they paid. But unless there is an expectation of dividend payments somewhere down the line, then the shares will be impossible to sell. To put it another way, if the boss of a company made an announcement that no more dividend payments would be made ever again, then the value of the shares in that company would instantaneously become zero. It is important to note, however, that if a new law was suddenly introduced that shares in a company could not be sold for any more than they were purchased for, their value would not go to zero. They would remain a perfectly viable investment on the basis that dividends could be earned from them.

Most people deny that rising stock prices are even part of what inflation should be measuring. Their reasoning is that stock price rises are merely an indicator that business is going well. For example, if you had shares in a shoe manufacturer and then that manufacturer invented a new machine for making shoes more efficiently then they would make more profits and be able to pay out higher dividends to their shareholders and so their share price would rise. Measuring this rise and calling it inflation would be nonsensical. Inflation should be measuring a price rise for a given fixed good. If, during some period of time, that good becomes inherently more valuable (like the shoe company with the better machine) then comparing the price at the end to the price at the beginning would not be inflation. It would be like comparing the price of an 8 ounce bar of chocolate at the end of the year to the price of a 4 ounce bar at the beginning of the year and announcing that there had been 100% inflation!

At this point you may be thinking that there is no point, and perhaps no meaning, in attempting to identify "inflation" in share prices, but this is not the case. In this section we hope to demonstrate that share price inflation is a) possible, b) measurable and c) powerfully predictive of economic catastrophes.

Coming back to the shoe-making company for a moment; imagine that the invention of the new machine essentially doubled the expected future dividend payments. Logically, this should cause a doubling of the share price. And indeed if that share price doubled, then this should not be considered an indication of any inflation at all. But what if the share price instead tripled?... Now things are different. The expected future dividends as a fraction of the share price have gone down; or to put it another way, the share price as a multiple of the expected dividend payments has gone up. The shares are now poorer value. There has been real inflation in those shares. At this point some may say, "Okay, so in theory you can measure share price inflation, but in practice it is going to be impossible because it's going to be far too difficult to measure expected future dividends for a company." This may be true if we are looking at individual companies, but when averaged over all the companies in an entire stock market then the problem becomes more tractable. Indeed this research has already been done.

A digression on the price–earnings ratio

When considering buying shares in a company, arguably the most important thing to consider is the ratio of the price of the shares to your estimate of future earnings or dividend payments. This estimate may be very hard to make, especially for new and/or small companies. New companies tend not to make any profits at all in their early years. But for large, established companies there may well be a relatively stable track record of earnings to consider. Investors often quote the ratio of the current share price to the earnings made by the company in the previous year as the *price–earnings ratio* or *PE ratio*.

PE ratio = Price of a share / Earnings made in previous year

Professor Robert Shiller of Yale University studied the PE ratios of the (generally large and established) companies in the Standard and Poor's index (S&P 500). Shiller knew full well that only looking at "last year's earnings" was not a great predictor of future dividends payments due to short-term fluctuations, so he instead used an average taken over the previous ten years (with some corrections for CPI inflation) creating a "PE10" measure. See Figure 5-4 for the PE10 of the S&P 500 since 1881.

Figure 5-4 Shiller's PE10 data.

The long-term average value of PE10 has been around 15, so perhaps we could deduce that a PE10 of 15 corresponds to reasonable and sustainable value. Any time that the PE10 value rises significantly above 15 it is an indication that something strange and unsustainable is happening. With an individual company, purchasing shares when the PE ratio is very high, or even infinite (i.e. when no earnings have been made yet), is not necessarily a bad thing. If the company has not been going very long and has yet to make any dividend payments then, so long as its business plan is good, it may well make high profits (and hence high dividend payments) in the future. Perhaps even with an established company, if it has recently broken into a new market or invented some new, improved manufacturing process then perhaps its share price deserves to be far higher than its PE ratio might indicate. But (and it's a big but) it is very hard to make an argument like this for an entire stock market. Look at the PE10 ratio for the S&P 500 in 1929 just before the onset of the Great Depression. It reached over 30. To have such a ratio would imply that the average expected future profitability of all 500 companies in the S&P 500 would be double its long-term norm. This expectation of massive profitability across all industry was not supportable by any logic and sure enough share prices came crashing down shortly after. Amazingly the entire episode repeated itself with the dot com boom. Shiller's data was available for all to see, but was studiously ignored.

In conclusion, there can indeed be inflation in the price of shares but it needs to be measured by looking at the price relative to the PE10 ratio of a basket of large established companies: i.e. if PE10 is rising then there is inflation in share prices; if PE10 is falling then there is deflation.

Visualising money circulation

Many economics textbooks include diagrams to show how money flows within an economy. The diagrams almost invariably show the different groups (banks, industry, government etc.) in fixed locations with the money flowing from one group to another. While these diagrams may be useful in some senses, they usually fail to convey some important characteristics of money flows.

In this section we will present an unconventional way of thinking about the flow of money. Imagine the act of money being used to purchase a good or service (hereafter given the single label "good" for simplicity) to be akin to two people crossing the road in opposite directions. Imagine the money starting out on the left-hand side of the road and the good being purchased starting out on the right. The exchange occurs when the money passes the good heading in the opposite direction. The money and the good will always cross in pairs at the same time. Now imagine this on a larger scale. You could visualise all the transfers of money for goods in the entire economy being carried out on a long stretch of road, with all the money that exists lined up on the left-hand side and all the items ready for sale lined up on the right. You could now observe a series of paired-up "swaps" of money for goods occurring along the road.

One apparent problem with this visualisation is that, as stated so far, all the money that exists would end up on the right-hand side of the road and no money would be left for any further purchasing. We can fix this by simply imagining some underpass whereby money can instantly travel from the right-hand side of the road back to the left, so that all the money that exists is always available to be used for purchasing.

The visualisation is far from complete, but it is useful to pause and consider what we have so far. See Figure 5-5.

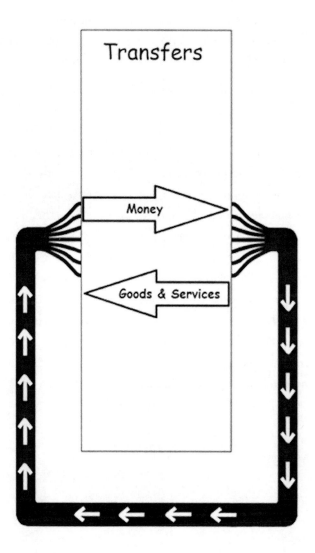

Figure 5-5 A (too) simple model of money flows.

This simple mental model appears to be the basis of many theories about money flows and inflation. For example, the diagram makes it clear that the flow of money mirrors the flow of goods. This "mirroring" can be expressed mathematically in the *equation of exchange* (MV=PT) which you will see described in almost all economics textbooks. This equation states that the amount of money in the economy (M) times its rate of flow (V) equals the rate of sales of goods (T) multiplied by the average price of those goods (P).

Unfortunately this visualisation of money flows as described so far is slightly too simple. It has led to some serious errors and confusion. A more correct model requires the inclusion of a variety of additional money flows. This risks making the diagram rather complex, so for clarity the goods flowing from right to left are not shown. Take a look at Figure 5-6. This new model now incorporates money creation and destruction. The creation of money occurs as banks make new loans. Money gets destroyed as the principal on those loans gets repaid to banks. The model also incorporates money flows which are used in relation to financial instruments such as shares and bonds, both money used to *purchase* the instruments and well as money *paid out from* those instruments such as dividend or coupon payments. This diagram also includes money used for loan interest repayments. Note that, unlike purchasing goods, loan repayments are not paired up with items flowing in the opposite direction; they are simply "fulfilling obligations".

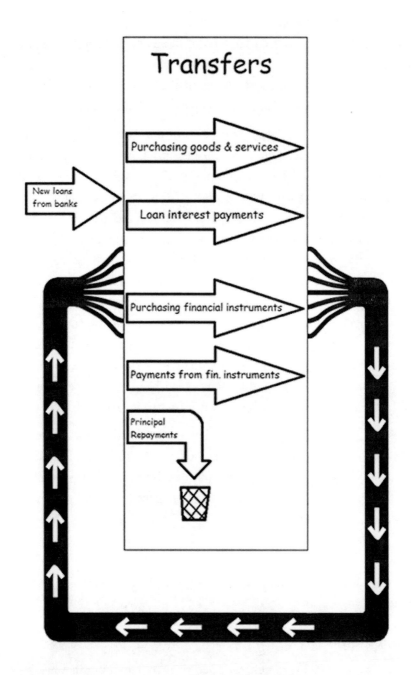

Figure 5-6 A more realistic model of money flows.

From this more complete model you can now see that the money in the economy is busy doing all sorts of things other than purchasing goods and services. The money supply has to share its flow rate between all these different activities. If there is more flow going to one activity there will clearly be less for everything else.

They key thing to note is what fraction of the money flows is being used for purposes related to the various inflation indices compared to money being used for other purposes which have little to do with the production of goods and services. If this fraction expands over some period then inflation (as measured by the CPI index, for example) will be high even if the total money supply is constant. Conversely if this fraction shrinks then inflation will be negative (deflation) even if the total money supply is constant. And confusingly if the changes in this fraction occur at a faster rate than any changes in the money supply, then you can have a state called *biflation* where there may be inflation occurring at the same time as a fall in the money supply, or deflation with a rising money supply. Few economists understand or have even heard of the concept of biflation and they may get very confused when it is occurring.

Another feature of money flows that we hope this diagram helps illustrate is that money is almost never held for any significant period by anyone, even when people *think* that are simply holding on to money. For example, when someone goes to "store" money in the bank, the bank will almost immediately use that money, either to buy a financial instrument like a share or bond or to lend it to someone. Money is like a "hot potato" that nobody wants to hold on to. Almost none of it will ever stay in one place for any significant time.

Conclusion

If you want to measure general price rises of "anything that can be purchased by anyone" then it is essential to include house prices and prices of financial instruments, otherwise you can be misled. Some economists suggest that it is better to just measure changes in the money supply directly and define that as inflation.

6 Booms and Busts – the Austrians Were on the Right Track

Economic development around the world has been punctuated by many periods of what appear to be "booms" followed by "busts". The *booms* are often characterised by relatively full employment in combination with sharply rising prices of some particular asset class, often housing or shares. This is often referred to as an *asset bubble*. The *busts* can be characterised by a sharp fall in the asset price that had previously been rising, combined with high levels of unemployment.

This chapter will explain the underlying causes of these phenomena. The ideas proposed here are inspired by, but not identical to, Austrian Business Cycle Theory, a collection of ideas proposed by the Austrian School of economics.

The Austrian School of economics
The Austrian School of economics is so named because some of its early founders happened to be Austrian, though as time went on its supporters came to be found all over the world. Indeed the current centre for promoting its teachings, The Ludwig von Mises Institute, is located in the US. Austrian economists could perhaps be described as the ultimate "free market fundamentalists". Their answer to almost every conceivable economic issue is "leave it to the free market". They assume this will naturally lead to the optimal outcome for all. This book does not subscribe to this view.

The boom

This section will describe the mechanics of the boom phase of the business cycle. This phase is often misdiagnosed because the high price of the asset concerned is usually driven by two components acting at the same time.

The seeds of an asset bubble

The seed of a boom is very often a clear and sustained rise in the price of some asset class (typically shares or houses), usually for a genuine fundamental reason to do with supply and demand. For the sake of argument, in the coming parts of this discussion we shall refer to this initial rise as being caused by "Reason X". This is the first of the two components that drive the price rise. The second is more complex, and requires a little digression before it can be introduced.

Trading on margin and its cousin, the mortgage

The next ingredient in the recipe for creating bubbles, concerns a mechanism used by speculators known as *trading on margin* and an economically similar device, the mortgage. Trading on margin is a trick employed to make greater profits from a successful investment. It works as follows:

Trading on margin

Imagine a speculator is confident that the price of an asset is going to rise strongly over the next year. As an example, say that the asset is shares in General Motors. Let us also say that he has $1,000 to invest. The speculator can profit from this prediction by simply using his money to purchase the asset, wait a year, then sell up and pocket the difference. If the shares rose by 15% he would have a profit of $150.

There is, however, a way to boost his earnings. What he can do is borrow some money for his investment. Say he borrowed $10,000 at 5% interest. Now he would have $11,000 to buy GM shares.

One year later he can sell the shares for 15% more, i.e. $1,650.

Now he has to pay the 5% interest on the loan. This will be $500.

So the net profit over the year will be $1,150, far greater than the $150 without the loan.

This method of magnifying your potential profits is a form of financial *leverage*. The degree of leverage is expressed as the ratio of the amount of loaned money to the amount of money the investor has available himself for the investment, so in this example the leverage is 10:1.

Trading on margin is considered a high-risk strategy because if your prediction turns out wrong and the shares go down in value then potentially you can lose more than your original investment. This kind of investment strategy is less common among small individual investors but is almost routine among fund managers and other large institutions.

Note that for trading on margin to work profitably, the increase in the price of the asset must outstrip the interest rate being charged for the loan. So increases in interest rates will reduce the propensity for investors to employ this technique.

Getting a mortgage in order to buy a house for investment purposes has very similar economic characteristics to trading on margin. The investment in this case is the house. The investor's contribution is the deposit and the remaining money is made up by the loan. If the price of the house rises at a faster rate than the interest on the loan then the profit that the householder can make on their investment can be far greater than that which they could make had they only been able to invest their original deposit.

Both trading on margin and buying houses as an investment can be summarised as follows:

> **People who are confident in the rising price of an asset may like to borrow money in order to invest it in that asset.**

The word "may" in that sentence depends on how confident the investor is that the price of the asset will rise faster than the rate of interest on the money that needs to be borrowed. We can now make a more accurate summation of the situation:

> **People who are confident in the rising price of an asset may like to borrow money in order to invest it in that asset. The greater their confidence in the rise and the lower the interest rate, the greater the enthusiasm for this process.**

There is one more key fact that needs to be considered here. In Chapter 1 we learned how loans *create* money. So we can further modify the summation as follows:

> **When people are confident that an asset can rise in price at a rate greater than the current interest rate then fresh new money will be created for the purposes of purchasing those assets. The greater the confidence in the rise and the lower the interest rate, the greater the enthusiasm for this process.**

Simple supply and demand will tell you that the more money there is chasing an asset, the higher the price will go. We can now state that:

> **More money being created for the purposes of purchasing this class of asset pushes up the price. This in turn creates more confidence that the price will continue rising.**

This constitutes a *positive feedback* loop in the asset price. As discussed earlier, an asset bubble can get started when there is a sustained rise in the price of an asset for a fundamental reason. When people observe this rise for a long enough period, their confidence in its continued rise will grow. This will give people the confidence to trade on margin and the feedback loop can then kick in and the bubble will grow. Sadly so few people know of the feedback loop that many commentators will ascribe *all* of the rise to Reason X even though this was merely the seed.

Delusions of future wealth

With the steadily rising price of the asset class (rising at a rate faster than would be caused by Reason X alone) owners of that asset can foolishly believe that they will have greater wealth in the future than they will have in reality. The bubble is certain to burst. This delusion of future wealth leads to a wide variety of economic "errors".

The Austrians talk about "malinvestments" during the boom phase, though this gives too much emphasis on the *investment* decisions of entrepreneurs. The phenomenon is more generalised than that. The errors are being made by almost everyone. People's spending decisions, their propensity to save, the types of business that will flourish, the types of business that will diminish or fail, as well as the investment choices of banks will all be affected by the erroneous optimism about future wealth. So perhaps we should state that during the boom phase there will be a combination of "malinvestments" as well as "malspending".

The bust

One can consider the price of an asset as being made up of two components:

1. a price based on the inherent desirability of the asset on its own merits

2. a premium over and above "Price 1", based purely upon expectations that you will be able to sell the asset at a higher price at some future point.

During an asset bubble the second component will grow and grow while the first component may remain relatively unchanged. This is what we have seen time and time again, either in the form of unsustainably high share prices (see Shiller's PE10 data from Figure 5-4), house prices, or more recently, in the price of derivatives.

As many economists have pointed out, "If something cannot go on forever, it won't." When the price of an asset class has been rising steadily for some initial period, many people may assume that it is bound to continue rising and they will merrily invest in the asset, thereby raising prices in the bubble. But there will eventually, possibly years after the start, come a point where the price of the asset becomes so obviously unsustainable that more and more people begin to become sceptical that it can go any further. At some point the sceptics will begin to outnumber the "believers" and the prices will turn around. As soon as this starts to happen then the aforementioned "Premium over Price 1" will vanish. The positive feedback loop then acts to accelerate the price change in the opposite direction, i.e. people see the prices falling and they no longer want to hold on to the asset so they sell, or at least are reluctant to buy. This signals prices to go down... and so on and so on.

An end to the rise at some point is guaranteed but there will always be *some* event that people will claim was the cause, even if it was merely the straw that broke the camel's back.

At this point let's remind you of the two phenomena discussed earlier:

- Borrowing causes money creation (via fractional reserve banking).

- Speculators like to borrow in order to invest in assets that they think will rise in price (trading on margin).

Obviously the price of the assets involved in the bubble are no longer expected to rise; quite the opposite, they are expected to fall. We now need to introduce the corollary to these phenomena:

- Paying back loans/defaulting causes money to disappear out of existence.

- Speculators who had recently been doing a lot of borrowing will now no longer have that desire. Indeed speculators whose investments have fallen in price dramatically may default on their loan repayments.

You should be able to see now that this scenario will naturally lead to a significant shrinking of the money supply. Indeed when the stock market bubble preceding the Great Depression burst, the money supply shrank by around a third. A big drop in the money supply has a whole host of bad side-effects, which we will come to later.

The faulty brakes on the positive feedback loop

Mainstream economics might suggest that there are natural brakes on the feedback loop that would prevent any runaway asset price boom from developing too far. The idea would be as follows:

A natural braking mechanism

1. If the money supply (due to all the trading on margin or mortgage lending) started growing too fast then this would show up as high inflation.

2. Governments instruct their central banks to use interest rates to keep inflation to a reasonably low level, commonly 2%.

3. If inflation started to rise then central banks will raise interest rates and it will become expensive to borrow money and the speculator's trick of borrowing money in order to invest will no longer be so attractive.

4. Asset prices will start to level off and the boom will be over before it has barely got started.

Step 2 of this braking system should sound familiar to you. It has been, and still is, an extremely popular policy implemented by governments throughout the world. Unfortunately there is a problem with this...

Why the brakes don't work very well

In practice this braking mechanism is flawed. The critical problem is the assumption that an increase in the money supply will directly lead to an increase in CPI inflation. If this assumption is incorrect then it may be possible for the money supply to increase without triggering significant immediate inflation and therefore without giving central banks the signal that they need to raise interest rates.

As already described in Chapter 5 it is indeed possible for CPI/RPI inflation to remain relatively low even when the money supply is increasing at a rapid rate. If the newly created money is being used for trading assets involved in the bubble that are not measured within the scope of the CPI then the CPI may appear to be relatively stable.

Higher prices in one sector do *not* quickly lead to higher prices in all sectors

Now you may argue that the higher prices of *any* specific asset class (shares, housing etc.) will soon feed into the rest of the economy and will cause more generalised price rises that will be picked up by textbook inflation measures. This is because the rises in these prices will eventually lead to the newly rich investors spending their money on everyday items like the rest of us, thereby signalling that prices should rise. But this process can be subject to very long delays. If, for example, the price rises are in shares, working to the benefit of a pension fund, then the bulk of the rise in prices is scarcely being spent in to the rest of the economy at all. There may some leakage in the system in as much as the flow of newly retiring people will gain, but the vast bulk of money sloshing around in the pensions system will remain doing nothing other than trading back and forth between different shares. Similarly, when wealthy investors, banks and hedge funds see that they are onto a good thing with a skyrocketing investment, the last thing they want to do is sell up and take the profit. They have a big incentive to leave their money in the system for as long as possible.

Economists from the Austrian School prefer to define inflation purely in terms of money supply growth. If this was the standard measure, and central banks had been instructed to use interest rates to keep *that* measure low, then none of the recent asset bubbles would have occurred, at least not to anything like the same degree.

The central banks never got a signal to raise interest rates

In relation to the recent sub-prime housing crisis, as mentioned earlier, a variety of central banks were instructed to target a CPI inflation rate of 2%. The CPI did not measure house price inflation in any way, not even mortgage repayments. So for years interest rates were set too low and people were taking out ever larger loans (creating new money) to buy houses. The price of houses inevitably went higher and higher. The majority of house buyers/owners did not spend much of the increased price of their houses into the rest of the economy. Sometimes the reverse would happen. People were straining so hard to join/stay on the housing bandwagon, spending so much of their income on mortgage repayments, that they would spend an ever decreasing fraction of their income on "normal" consumer goods, i.e. the kinds of things that would be measured by the CPI index. The result was that the government were blind to the creation of this bubble. They would "explain" the rise in house prices purely in terms of a shortage of housing or on increasing numbers of immigrants. Indeed the availability of some reasonable sounding explanations was part of the problem. The fact there were factors that would and should have led to *some* rise in house prices served only to fool so many politicians and economists into thinking that these factors explained *all, or almost all* of the rise.

Psychological effects of a boom–bust cycle

Some people seem to assume that asset bubbles are something that only concerns bankers, but this could not be further from the truth. Asset bubbles do a huge amount of harm to the real economy. The supposed good effects of the "boom" phase are more than offset by the bad effects of the "bust". We would all be far better off if there was no bubble at all.

Bad things happen on the way up...

When an asset bubble is in full swing, large numbers of people have unrealistically optimistic expectations of their future wealth because their investments appear to be growing in value at a galloping pace. They will develop corresponding patterns of spending/saving/borrowing. If the upswing of bubble happens over a long period then the economy will have gradually migrated to serve this pattern. Sectors catering to people under the delusion that they have great future wealth will have grown and will now be employing too many people. Industries catering to people with realistic expectations about their future wealth will have shrunk and will now be employing too few people. The industry involved in the bubble itself will be the most distorted of all. So if, for example, the bubble was in housing then obviously there will now be far too many builders, real estate agents and mortgage brokers. Whatever asset the bubble is in, the financial services sector will have become bloated with the profits from these excessive loans.

... and even worse things that happen on the way down

People's behaviour in the aftermath of an asset bubble is, not surprisingly, the opposite of what it was on the way up. The delusion about future wealth has now been corrected. People's patterns of spending/saving/borrowing will inevitably change. The sector involved in the bubble will be hit hard. The correction of this situation clearly involves the opposite migration of workers to that which occurred on the way up. Workers need to move away from both the sector involved in the bubble and the sectors over-manned due to the unsustainable patterns of spending/saving/borrowing. They need to migrate toward the rest of the economy, especially those sectors which became *undermanned* as a consequence of the distorted signals.

Unfortunately, unless we live in a "planned" economy where government dictates what jobs we have, the only way that this migration can take place is to allow the excess workers in the unsustainable sectors to lose their jobs and then be absorbed by the rest of the more conventional economy. This is a painful process but there is no way to avoid it. Unfortunately short-sighted governments, egged on by bad economists, will not realise what needs to happen and they will attempt to "prop up" or subsidise those unsustainably large sectors of the economy, with invariably bad results. Propping up unsustainably large sectors must, by definition, harm the process of getting more workers into the undermanned sectors. So there is a danger of ending up in a situation in which a too-small group of people producing goods that we all need have to subsidise a too-large group of people whose job it is to produce goods or services that nobody wants any more. Governments will describe this "propping up" as "saving jobs", whereas all that is happening is the prevention of the economy from correcting itself.

And the story does not end there. There are additional problems that emerge after the bursting of an asset bubble, which we will come to in the next chapter.

7 Monetary Illusions and Unemployment

In this chapter we will explore the idea that pessimism about future wealth combined with the use of money is a recipe for unemployment. We shall demonstrate, with a thought experiment, that if money is removed from the equation then the pessimism on its own does not lead to unemployment. The resulting insights may help us escape the "paradox of thrift", an idea popularised in modern times by John Maynard Keynes, though its roots date back very much earlier.

Unemployment types

The study of unemployment is a little messy because it is a problem that exists even in the best of times. In a perfectly thriving economy there will always be new technologies evolving, markets becoming saturated and tastes changing, all of which mean that people must occasionally change jobs from one sector to another, perhaps with some retraining involved. It is impractical to expect people to move from one job to another without spending at least some period being unemployed. Then there is the problem of certain people *choosing* to be unemployed because government-backed unemployment benefits have been set at a level which is perceived by some as comfortable enough to live on.

In this section we are not going to cover either of *those* types of unemployment. What we will discuss here is unemployment over and above that level: the kind of unemployment where normally hard-working people, perhaps people who have already worked for many years, suddenly cannot find any work. Or even the kind of underemployment where skilled people find themselves having to wait at tables or take part-time work because that is all they can find. We shall, for want of a better phrase, label this as *excess unemployment*.

Following the standard procedure of this book, let's first consider unemployment without money. At first glance it may seem that the use of money could have no possible impact on unemployment. But, perhaps surprisingly, there are major, purely monetary components to it. Before we can explore those, we have to consider the reasons for excess unemployment in the first place.

When do we have high unemployment?

The most obvious periods in which we have excess unemployment is after the bursting of some kind of asset bubble. Large sectors of the economy (house building, for example) have been exposed as being overmanned. Companies in these sectors will start to fail. A wave of new unemployment will occur for this reason alone.

Additionally the value of people's savings, whether that be tied up in the value of their houses or the value of their pension funds, has now been exposed as being far lower than had previously been assumed. The population at large is being given a message: "Your savings are inadequate." Quite naturally and rationally there is a rapid aggregate shift from unsustainable profligacy to a new desire to save. Everyone, not just individuals but also government departments and businesses, will now feel the need to cut back on their spending. The consequences of this shift in behaviour will be considered next with the aid of some thought experiments.

Pessimism in a world without money

Let's now consider what would happen in an economy hit by a sudden desire to save that did not have money. For the purposes of this thought experiment, the model society must very *strictly* be without money. An ordinary vanilla barter economy will not suffice because there will be goods that can act as a kind of money, perhaps gold or jewels. So just for the sake of argument, let us say that we have a "super-barter" world where there is no gold, no jewels and no high-value non-perishable commodities stores of value that can act as a money substitute or savings conduit.

It must be noted that the business cycle mechanism, described in Chapter 6, cannot occur in a super-barter economy, so we will have to invent some other reason for pessimism in our experiment. Let's say that a newspaper article had just been published stating that a famous soothsayer has just predicted hard times in the coming years due to floods, pestilence or the like. This soothsayer had always been right in the past and there is now widespread concern. People may think to themselves, "I'd better save up for the hard times ahead! I'll carry on working hard, perhaps working even harder than before, and at the same time I'll consume as little as possible so that I will have an excess of produce that I can use for savings."

Consider what options will be open to people in this state. We have already eliminated the possibility of the concentrated value storage savings mechanism (there is no gold or jewels by definition in this thought experiment), so the remaining options are simple warehouse and contract. Simple warehouse saving are of course extremely inefficient, so there will not be much enthusiasm for that. This leaves one last option, namely contract savings. Unfortunately this needs a willing partner to take the opposite side of that deal. Given all the pessimism about the future, there are going to be very few people willing to take the other side of that deal without driving hard bargains. The borrowers will be able to say, "You give me a *large amount* of your produce now in return for a *small amount* of my produce in the future." As the few remaining people willing to borrow do their deals, there will be fewer and fewer left, driving harder and harder bargains. This avenue of savings will soon become ostensibly blocked. All the savings mechanisms have evaporated, leaving no reasonable savings mechanisms available to anyone.

Now let's consider what will happen with production and trade in this pessimistic environment with no possibility of saving. Obviously people are still going to be working to manufacture as much as they can, but what will they do with their produce? It is impractical to store it for the long term; they have no option but to either consume it directly themselves, *at that time*, or use it to exchange for other people's produce, *at that time*. When they find people to exchange their goods with, both sides will have the usual incentives to receive as much as possible in return for their produce. So as you should now be able to see there is no reason, no incentive, no possibility to consume less than you produce despite the fact that there is a desire to. The people may *wish* they could save more, they may well be cursing the fact that they can't, but it will be clear to everyone that all the savings avenues have been used up. They may as well carry on consuming. We can sum this situation up as follows:

> **Pessimism about the future cannot lead to a significant reduction in consumption in a super-barter economy.**

Pessimism in a world with money

Now we shall consider what happens when money is introduced. Again, a wave of pessimism about the future strikes the population. Everybody wants to save. But now, with money available, people *think* they can save simply by storing their money. They think to themselves, "If I cut back on buying things with my money then I can store it in the bank and use that for when the hard times come." Unfortunately, and quite unlike the situation in the barter economy, this now *does* mean that consumption can decrease.

> **Pessimism about the future *can* lead to a significant reduction in consumption in a money-based economy.**

This will soon start a feedback loop. As people generally consume less, they will find it harder to sell the goods that they have made. Some people may find certain goods so hard to sell that their businesses go bust. They will lose their jobs. Other people, upon seeing their neighbours losing their jobs, will become even more concerned about the future and will try even harder to cut back on their consumption, causing even more people to lose their jobs. This feedback loop can be quite devastating for an economy.

The end of the spiral

Just in case you were wondering, the downward spiral of job losses does not go on forever. It may go down a long way and be pretty painful, but there is a bottom. The bottom is determined largely by what people decide they will cut back on. Obviously great swathes of the population will cut back on things that they consider luxuries, but the demand for things considered necessities will always remain. So when people have cut back on everything they think they can cut back on, a bottom will have been reached. No *further* people will be losing their jobs. Once people can see that the contraction in the economy has ceased, or is slowing down, then people will no longer think that they have to cut back any further. The feedback loop can now go into reverse and a recovery can begin.

The job losses after a bubble-bursting can thus be considered as having two components:

- the reverse-migration component.
- the monetary (paradox of thrift) component.

The *reverse-migration* component is the job losses in the sectors that had became oversubscribed during the upswing of the bubble. Exactly which sectors these are will depend on exactly which asset class was involved in the bubble.

The *monetary* component is the unfortunate *additional* jobs lost due to everyone's desire to cut back on consumption. There will be a tendency for the job losses to be concentrated in sectors providing goods and services that people choose to cut back on when they are pessimistic about their future.

The jobs lost in the process of reverse migration should be seen as a positive thing for the economy, a correction of errors, whereas the jobs lost due to the monetary component simply constitute a loss of wealth, a missed opportunity to produce or supply goods and services.

In conclusion, the key to full employment is to maintain people's expectations of their future wealth at a constant and realistic level. Remember that any period in which expectations of future wealth are raised above what is realistic will *always* be followed by a job-losing correction. The business cycle mechanism sure does one heck of a lot of damage.

Another way of expressing this is to say that it is essential to maintain a balance between those in the economy that are keen to consume more than they produce and those that wish to produce more than they consume. At the time of writing there is an almost overwhelming desire to consume less than we produce in a great many countries and very few people wish to do the reverse. This is a perfect recipe for a downward spiral of the paradox of thrift-type unemployment.

Why major wars end depressive spirals

It has been noticed by many economists that wars appear to end depressions. The reason for this is that at the end of a war, when your cities are in ruins and the economy is on its knees, the balance between savers and borrowers shifts dramatically. In good times, lots of savings take place precisely for use on "a rainy day". When the city around you is in ruins, what could be more of a rainy day? Very few people are going to be saying to themselves, "I'd better start saving now in case there are some hard times ahead." These *are* the hard times. Naturally the general assumption will be that the future will be more prosperous than the present.

A mountain of debt is a constant source of pessimism

If there are high levels of debt after a bubble bursts this can leave an economy in a state from which it is very difficult to recover. Before the bursting of the bubble both individuals and governments may have chosen to run up debts which were towards the limits of repayability, i.e. they may have calculated that the interest on those debts was just about repayable given their predictions of future income and future growth of their investments. The bursting bubble now reveals their predictions were overoptimistic and their debts can become unrepayable. This may not be realised immediately. People may say to themselves, "These debts look pretty bad right now, but maybe things will get better and I could pay them back later. In the meantime I'll just cut back on my spending to try to keep up the interest payments." This plan serves only to suppress demand further.

Some economists have tried to suggest that an aggregate drop in demand is nonsensical because for every person in debt there must be a person to whom the debt is owed, so even though the debtor may be pessimistic and cutting back there must be a creditor gleefully collecting all this money and spending it, thereby keeping demand constant. This, however, is not the case. It will be clear to the creditors that the debtors are struggling. Many debtors will be late with their payments, and a few will start to default. The creditors will become concerned that the default problem will get worse in the future. The creditors are liable to become every bit as pessimistic as the debtors. The economy can be in a cul-de-sac from which there seems no escape.

The problem of too much unrepayable debt in an economy has been observed a great many times all over the world since antiquity. Indeed in biblical times there were regular debt jubilees where every few decades all debts would be officially cancelled. Professor Michael Hudson has written of this in his work *The Lost Tradition of Biblical Debt Cancellations*. Implementing ideas taken from biblical times may seem strange, but if the debts built up in an economy have grown too high, a jubilee or something like it may be the only way to avoid a Great Depression.

8 A Growing/Shrinking Money Supply: More Causes and Effects

Discussing the effect of changing money supply in isolation from other economic factors is difficult because in the real world the money supply so often changes in tandem with other events. So just for the sake of argument, let us tease out the money supply aspect of an economy with a thought experiment.

A money supply thought experiment

Let's assume that the economy is undergoing a relatively stable period. We are playing God (this is a thought experiment after all) and can increase or decrease the money supply at will, by magic. When we want to increase the money supply (let's say we want to double it), we will simply increase the amount of money everyone has simultaneously overnight, i.e. if you go to bed having $10 in your wallet, you will wake up with $20 the next morning. This will apply equally to electronically stored money, but importantly it won't affect financial agreements in any way. If you've signed a document saying that you owe someone $50, you will still owe them $50.

Under the conditions of this thought experiment, it is easy to imagine the effect on prices of a big jump in the money supply. Imagine that overnight the money supply increases tenfold. Now imagine you are the owner of an electrical goods store. When you open up the shop the next day, you notice a flood of gleeful customers excitedly buying up everything they can get their hands on. Using what we have learned from the section on supply and demand, it is clear that the shopkeepers would soon start raising their prices. Indeed it should be obvious that a new equilibrium would be reached in which the prices are approximately ten times what they had been previously.

Some aspects of economic activity are relatively immune to changes in the money supply. Consider produce that can be made from scratch in a short period by a flexible workforce where the chain from raw materials to final product is short and there is no expensive equipment used in the manufacturing process. These people can simply adjust their wages and prices up or down to suit the current level of money supply. If the money supply went up, they would increase both their prices and their wages; if it went down, they would decrease both their prices and their wages. The company is perfectly able to cope with the changes without significant disruption. Indeed the overall wealth of its employees in terms of their ability to purchase goods and services could remain approximately constant. Not all aspects of economic activity get off so lightly, however. The real problems arise with long-term loan arrangements:

An unexpected increase in the money supply

Say that Person A has made a long-term loan to Person B on the basis of a fixed interest rate. If the money supply unexpectedly increased during the loan repayment period, then B is delighted. It will become easier for them to gather together the money to pay back the loan. A, however, is hurt because the money they get back will have less purchasing power then they expected.

An unexpected decrease in the money supply

Say that Person A makes a loan to B for a car. At the time of the loan the borrower may think to themselves something like, "I just need to pay back 10% of my income each month and after a few years the car will be mine." Now comes the unexpected shrinking of the money supply. The person's numerical income will decrease (as will everyone else's and as will prices); they will now have to pay back a higher percentage of their income in order to keep up with the obligations of the loan. This higher percentage may be too much to bear, and there is a risk B may default. If B does succeed in paying back the loan then A is delighted. A may only get back the same numerical amount of money as they were originally expecting but now that same amount of money will have more purchasing power. Let's summarise the situation in a table:

Effects of money supply changes on fixed interest rate loan arrangements		
	Unexpected **increase** in the money supply	Unexpected **decrease** in the money supply
Lender (A)	**Worse off.** They will get back the predicted numerical amount of cash, but that cash will purchase less than they had hoped.	**Better off** *if* **he gets paid back.** May have option of seizing B's possessions.
Borrower (B)	**Better off.** They have to give back the same numerical amount of cash, but obtaining the cash will be easier than expected.	**Worse off.** More painful repayments. May have to forfeit their possessions (depending on the loan agreement).

Table 8-1 Effects of unexpected changes to the money supply.

This vandalism of loan and payback arrangements is generally a bad thing for an economy and generally bad politically. After all, everyone who is now worse off will be complaining bitterly, and some may even go bankrupt or lose their homes.

Unexpected changes in the money supply clearly cause great harm.

Mortgages are particularly sensitive to money supply changes

Let's consider one type of loan/repayment arrangement that is particularly sensitive to money supply changes, namely mortgages. If interest rates are held at a low rate for too long this can cause a rise in house prices, risking a house price bubble. The lower interest rates will mean that people will be able to afford larger mortgages. This corresponds to money creation, with the new money flowing into the housing sector. If this carries on for a sustained period people may think that prices will inevitably carry on rising. They will want to join the bandwagon and buy a new/bigger house too. This causes further rises in house prices and yet more people will want to join in, stretching themselves to the limit. The overall money supply will grow and grow during the years that this housing boom takes to pan out.

At some point people will be able to stretch no more without a further drop in interest rates. If that is not forthcoming then the upward march in house prices will cease and the business cycle mechanism will switch into reverse gear. The money supply will suddenly and "unexpectedly" (at least for most mainstream economists) start to contract. Governments now cannot stand to have the money supply shrink because people will find it harder to make their mortgage repayments, possibly resulting in them losing their homes. Banks may suffer because if people start to default then the banks go bust. As with the bursting of any asset bubble, people who had previously been under an illusion of great future wealth now realise that they were deluded and will be keen to save more and consume less. This causes job losses and a downward spiral as discussed earlier.

Governments throughout the world have repeatedly assumed that the only solution to this ugly situation is to a) lower interest rates and b) inject new money into the economy. They call this "stimulating" the economy. The idea is to achieve the following effects:

- Hope that the low interest rates will encourage bigger mortgages and so prevent a big fall in house prices.

- Prevent those with existing large mortgages from losing their homes.

- Help prevent the banks from going bust.

But there are problems with this "cure". It is attempting to prop up the previously wasteful scenario with too many real estate agents, too much house building and a too large financial sector.

Excessively low interest rates are a banking subsidy. They correspond to a continuous flow of wealth from society at large to banks. This props up a wastefully bloated financial sector, depriving the real economy of so much talent that could be employed more productively elsewhere.

Why excessively low interest rates are a subsidy to banks
At the time of writing (2011) we have ultra low interest rates in many countries. This means that commercial banks can borrow from their central banks at near enough 0% then invest in government bonds at a higher rate and pocket the difference. It's like a giant tap turned on, pouring money into the open mouths of bankers, all at the expense of the taxpayer.   This scenario is unfortunate because it is in a post-bubble period that the financial sector is exposed as being far too big. The government should be letting the sector lose jobs. These people should migrate to new jobs, doing something productive instead.

The bad side-effects of the "cure" are every bit as bad as the disease. The longer that interest rates are held at unreasonably low levels, the more people will get tied into oversized mortgages. This makes it ever more painful to raise interest rates in the future. Society can get locked in to low rates, painted into a corner.

An alternative solution to a post-housing-bubble depression

Before we describe the alternative solution, we need a quick digression on loan sharks...

120

Loan sharks exist in many if not all societies. They prey on the poorest, least educated people, offering loans to people they know may struggle to pay the money back. Their interest rates are exorbitantly high and so a few late or missed repayments can quickly lead to astronomical debts that can never be repaid, leaving the borrower a virtual slave to the lender, with the loan shark using threats of physical violence to collect repayments.

Loan shark debts are not normally enforceable in law. The idea is that loans made recklessly to people the lender knows will struggle to pay back is seen by society as an evil committed by the lender.

By the same logic that dictates that debts to loan sharks should not be enforceable, we would suggest that the solution to a bursting house price bubble would be to realise and accept that the financial sector, in combination with central banks, had been making reckless loans. Therefore repaying the full amount of the loans should not be enforceable. We would suggest that if someone had been given a mortgage of five or six times their annual income, based on the fact that interest rates just happened to be at some unusual and unsustainable low, then the law should step in and dictate that the borrower be held accountable for only an amount corresponding to a more reasonable multiple of their annual income, perhaps 2.5 or 3 times their income. The effects of this plan would be as follows:

The desire to "cut back" or "consume less than you produce" resulting from realising your house is not so valuable after all, would be countered by the fact that your mortgage costs will be lowered dramatically. House prices would collapse simultaneously, but this is a good thing.

Many banks will go bust or be forced to downsize because the income from mortgage interest will be far smaller. This is a good and necessary thing because the banking sector was previously wastefully large. The money supply will certainly shrink in the process, but this could be replaced with debt-free base money created by the government.

9 Interest Rates and Investing Against Our Will

In order to better understand the how and why of interest rates it is revealing to consider interest rates in a barter society and then consider how things behave with the introduction of money. The idea of an interest rate even existing in a barter system may sound like a contradiction in terms, but it is actually perfectly possible.

Interest rates in a barter economy

Imagine a primitive society where much of the labour is tied up in the process of simply collecting enough food to eat. Also imagine that they have the technology to make non-perishable food, let's say salted fish. The society is organised enough so that all the citizens pool their spare food and place it in the hands of a wise and trusted person, the world's first "banker". The idea is people can be "loaned" food so that they can temporarily be relieved of the burden of having to find food for themselves. This enables them to carry out some project, like building a house or a boat. People can approach the banker and ask to "borrow" some of the food (we say borrow, but of course they will consume it and have to pay back *new* salted fish, which they will either catch themselves or obtain by bartering goods they make in the future). This system is a full-reserve system in as much as no two people can ever claim to own the same fish at a single instant: there are no cheques or tokens of ownership of fish, only the fish itself. People who save their fish with the banker tell him how long he is allowed to lend it out before they want it (or a replacement) back and the banker keeps this in mind when making loans.

The banker will charge some kind of interest rate, i.e. will insist that the borrower pay back all the fish plus some extra amount that would be profit shared between the banker and the community. Assuming that the banker wishes to maximise this profit, what interest rate should he charge?

The banker's best option is to adjust his advertised interest rate to exactly balance the supply and demand for loans. As demonstrated in Chapter 3, the banker will aim to tweak the interest rates such that all his possible loans are taken up, but only just. If he sets it too high then not all of the spare food will get lent out. If he sets it too low then the food will very quickly get lent out, but new borrowers will still be coming into the bank asking for loans and the banker will have to turn them away.

To summarise:

> In a barter system, interest rates will be adjusted to balance the supply and demand for loans.

Interest with money in a fractional reserve banking system

Now let's consider what would happen if instead of storing their spare salted fish with the wise and trusted person, the same society switched to using money, cheques and fractional reserve banking. What would happen to the supply and demand for loans then?

Presumably the characteristics of the *demand* for loans would be unchanged; after all, it's the same people with the same list of projects that they'd like to pursue. But now the characteristics of the *supply* of loans are completely different. The amount of money that can be supplied has the potential to be much larger than the amount of money that the society gave to the banker by way of savings. Exactly what happens next is subject to all sorts of complications, but for the moment let us consider three possible interest rates that the banker could choose to charge:

- **Barter rate:** The banker could choose exactly the same rate as had been determined under the barter system. This was the rate that led to people borrowing an amount equal to what was being saved, i.e. the total spending power of all the cheque books handed out would be approximately equal to enough money to purchase the salted fish that the community wished to save.

- **Greater than barter rate:** The banker could choose a higher rate of interest than the barter rate. This would deter people from borrowing and lead to less money being lent out than society had saved, i.e. the total spending power of all the cheque books handed out would amount to less than enough to purchase the salted fish that the community wished to save.

- **Less than barter rate:** The banker could choose a lower rate of interest than the barter rate. This would encourage people to borrow and lead to more money being lent out than society had saved, i.e. the total of all the spending limits of all the cheque books that were handed out would amount to more than enough to purchase the salted fish that the community wished to save.

Now clearly the barter rate and higher are both perfectly possible; no laws of physics are being broken. But the less than barter rate seems perplexing at first glance. How could banks lend out more than was being saved? This *does* sound like breaking the laws of physics! But it *can* all be resolved. The lending of "money" (cheque books with spending limits) over and above barter rate corresponds to a newly expanded money supply and will naturally lead to inflation. This inflation decreases the spending power of the money held by the community. It's almost as if the community were paying a kind of tax. The community is forfeiting part of its spending power. This loss of spending power of the community corresponds to the new spending power of the "excess" borrowers, i.e. the extra people who got loans over and above that which would have been lent out under the barter system.

Setting a too low interest rate is effectively forcing the community, against its will, to make these extra loans. The inflation deprives them of real goods and services which are instead being purchased by the excess borrowers. This is a subtle mechanism that the community may not even realise is going on.

So now that we know that all three options are available to the banker, and none of them break the laws of physics, we need to ask what rate the banker will actually choose. Because the supply of money for lending has the potential to expand enormously, the banker is no longer constrained by the normal forces of supply and demand. Instead the banker only need consider whether he can make a profit on the loans.

With fractional reserve banking, interest rates are *not* set to balance the supply and demand for loans. Instead they are a politically controlled tool that determines the amount of lending that can occur in an economy. The interest rate can be adjusted such that the amount of borrowing that occurs can be set to lower than, the same as or higher than society would naturally choose to lend out had it been left to its own devices.

This idea is not new. Indeed it is one of the cornerstones of Austrian economics. The ability of bankers (in conjunction with governments) to effectively set the amount of lending to above or below what society is naturally willing to save is not necessarily a bad thing in and of itself. If, for example, society had an inclination to save too little then industry may suffer from a lack of investment, and the society as a whole would suffer in the long term. It could potentially be a good thing for the government to force more savings. Having said that, it is also true that the ability for excess lending to take place has the potential to do great harm and so would need to be controlled with great skill and care. Sadly, perhaps more skill and care than most governments are capable of delivering.

In conclusion

Bankers have every incentive to do as much lending as they can make a profit from rather than simply lending out what has been saved by society. This fact leads to many interesting behaviours on the part of bankers which we shall explore in the following chapters.

10 Investments and Pseudo-investments: Which do Banks Prefer?

Listening to politicians, economists and bankers may well lead observers to believe the following:

- Bank lending is "investment".

- "Investments" help the economy grow.

- The more "investing" that happens, the wealthier we'll all be.

If these were all true then the fact that banks have an incentive to lend to as many people as possible for as many things as possible would be just fine. Their incentives would be perfectly aligned with what's best for the economy as a whole. We'd have a win-win situation... but there is a problem. While there is an element of truth in each of the statements, in the current era of modern banking it turns out they are all more false than true. In this chapter we will examine why.

True investments

Let us be clear about what constitutes a true investment. Here are some examples:

- Lending to an existing business so that it can buy a new machine for its factory. This machine will produce widgets (whatever it is they manufacture) more efficiently than their existing machine and so increase output and company profits.

- Lending money to an entrepreneur so that they can start a new business. They need the loan in order to buy raw materials and pay staff in the early stages of the company before it starts to make a profit.

- Lending money to a company for it to research a new manufacturing process.

- Lending money to a company for it to build a new factory.

These things are all quite clearly investments. These things are exactly what banks *should* be involved in.

Non-productive "investments" (pseudo-investments)

Consider a loan to someone for them to buy a holiday or some new furniture. Is *that* investment? Maybe it's a matter of definition. Maybe according to some economic dictionary somewhere it is classed as an "investment". After all, so long as the borrower pays the money back with interest, the lender will have made a profit. So from the lender's perspective it looks just the same as any other type of investment. You lend money out, you get a greater sum back. But clearly there is a difference. The true investments in the last section are designed to lead directly to an increase in productivity, whereas lending for a holiday or new furniture is clearly non-productive. One may argue that perhaps a holiday, or some more comfortable furniture, would lead to the recipient being able to work just that little bit more efficiently in their job, but the effect is very much secondary and is likely to be on a lesser order of magnitude than a true investment. Perhaps it could be said that a loan for a holiday was 5% productive, 95% non-productive. Even so, compared to a true productive investment, loans for holidays are extremely inefficient for increasing production.

It is interesting to note that in most countries there is nothing contained within banking regulations or the tax system that distinguishes productive from non-productive investments. Indeed there isn't even a separate word for non-productive investments in the standard economics textbooks! The books make almost no effort to distinguish between the two phenomena. We've even had to invent our own word for non-productive investments: we've called them *pseudo-investments*.

Governments around the world perceive investments as a) good for the economy and b) involving the lenders risking their money. Because of this they often take steps to encourage investment by giving tax breaks on profits from them. Governments will rarely distinguish investments from pseudo-investments in this regard.

Investments v. pseudo-investments: which do banks prefer?

There are many economists and politicians who insist that the "free market" is always best for an economy. Whatever people (or banks, or businesses) choose to do, based purely on their own selfish interests, is always perfectly aligned with what is best for society as a whole – this is Adam Smith's "invisible hand". The basis of laissez-faire economics. Margaret Thatcher, Ronald Reagan and George Bush were all keen advocates of this philosophy.

In this section we will analyse the process of a bank choosing between two loans to see whether it is deciding between them in society's best interests. For the sake of simplicity, let's imagine a fixed money supply system of banking with time deposits. With this type of banking, a bank cannot create money, and so will have strictly limited supplies. Imagine the bank is down to its last $10,000 of lendable funds for that day, and two competing borrowers enter the bank, both of whom wish to borrow the full $10,000 and both of whom are respected and trusted individuals whom the banker has every faith will pay back the loan plus interest.

Comparing two productive loans

First of all let's consider the case where both potential customers want the money for productive purposes.

Just to make the explanation simpler, imagine that the idea in both cases is for the borrower to buy new, faster, more efficient machines for their factories that will produce whatever it is they manufacture more efficiently than ever before (they are not necessarily manufacturing the same items).

So long as the banker has confidence that the loans will be repaid, the only consideration in determining who gets the loan is who is willing to pay the highest level of interest. Now assume that both potential borrowers have equally good advisors who have made equally accurate (or equally inaccurate) forecasts about the improved profitability that will be brought about by the loans. The man whose investment leads to the greatest rise in profitability will be able to afford the highest interest rate. This man will "win" the contest and get the loan.

Now we need to look at the benefits to all concerned in this lending process. The main benefits of a productive loan are made up from two parts, A and B, defined below:

Investments and Pseudo-investments: Which do Banks Prefer?

Benefit A	The benefit to the borrower in increased profits after the new machine is purchased.
Benefit B	The benefit to the community from having cheaper goods available to purchase as a result of the completed investment.

Table 10-1 Who benefits from a loan.

Benefit A is pretty obvious to anyone, but B may need a little explanation. You may suspect that when a company invests in new improved machinery that it may decide to simply keep its prices unchanged and enjoy the greater profits. This is indeed possible but in practice is rare. As long as the company is in competition with others it will usually be more profitable for it to lower its prices (as it is now more able to do) and take market share from its rivals. Additionally if the new, faster, more efficient machinery is available to all, then its rivals may also be purchasing it and so the forces of competition will surely drive the prices lower. Indeed the amount that the prices drop will in general be proportional to, or at least correlate with, A.

Now back to the banker's choice. We have seen that the banker is most likely to choose the borrower that can make the greatest increase in profits for themselves, i.e. the banker will choose the one with the highest value of component A. But we have also seen that the B component is likely to be proportional to A. Therefore we can conclude that the banker is indirectly going to select the investment with the highest value of B; the banker will be maximising the benefit to the community.

When comparing two productive loans, a banker will choose the one that gives the greatest benefit to society.

This result looks like confirmation of the principle of free market fundamentalism. Letting people act in their own selfish interests by a happy accident simultaneously results in the maximum benefit to society as a whole. A victory for the invisible hand!

Comparing a productive loan to a non-productive one

Let's now imagine a scenario in which two potential borrowers come into the bank, both wanting the bank's remaining $10,000. Both are well-respected, reliable people who, the banker is confident, will repay the loan plus interest. But now this time, one is after a productive loan like buying new machinery for his factory, and the other wants to build an extension to his house so that he can install a pool table. Again we must consider the major potential benefits to everyone affected by the transactions:

For the productive loan we have benefits A and B as before.

For the non-productive loan we have only the benefits to the borrower. A bit like A, except that the benefits are in terms of the enjoyment of the house extension rather than in terms of profits. Benefit B is far smaller than is the case for a productive loan.

Now let's consider what this looks like from the bank's perspective. Again the bank will give the loan to the person willing to pay the highest interest rate. This will be the one who perceives that the benefit to them personally will be greatest.

Now we can see that there is a fundamental difference between this choice and the one where both loans were productive. Imagine that the two borrowers' perceived benefits (to themselves) are rather similar. In this case what they are willing to pay in terms of interest would be a close run thing. Imagine that the man asking for the productive loan is willing to pay 9% and the man wanting the non-productive loan is willing to pay 9.001%. The banker, acting in his own selfish interests, will give the loan to the man asking for the non-productive loan. The banker has no reason to consider B, the benefit to society of the cheaper goods.

So in answer to the original question, "Real investments v. pseudo-investments: Which do banks prefer?", the answer is that they don't care. They will simply end up selecting the borrower who perceives the greatest benefit to *themselves*. The invisible hand fails to work in this scenario.

> **When comparing a productive loan to a non-productive loan, a banker will *not* necessarily choose the one that gives the greatest benefit to society.**

Is a productive loan *always* better than a non-productive one?

A productive loan is *usually* better for society as a whole than a non-productive one, though it is not guaranteed to always be so. If the benefit to a borrower for a non-productive purpose is very large compared to the size of the loan then this may be a "better" thing to do than arrange for a poor-quality productive loan which gives only a small benefit to society as a whole. Don't forget that the borrower is part of society too and we must not discount the personal benefit to them when we attempt to tot-up the *total* benefit of the loan.

Productive v. non-productive loans in a fractional reserve system

So we've seen that bankers do not take into account the total benefit to society of potential loans. So far the simplified scenarios used to demonstrate this result have been rather artificial and have involved a fixed money supply system of banking. When we come to translate this result to the real world we have to consider a fractional reserve system where it is perfectly possible for banks to lend out a greater sum of money than people have saved. It all depends on the interest rate that gets charged; this is at least partially controlled by the actions of a central bank.

Imagine the collection of all the people in society that would want to take out a loan, given a low enough rate of interest. Some might want the loans for a productive purpose; some may want them for something non-productive. Now imagine lining them all up, ranked in order of who is willing to pay the highest level of interest. Then imagine the assorted levels of interest that the banks could charge. If the rate was very high then only a small fraction of those people at the front of the line would end up taking out loans. If the rate was set lower then a greater fraction of these people in the line would end up taking out loans. Under most circumstances (except in the aftermath of an asset bubble bursting) the government, in cooperation with the central banks, will usually not want everyone who wants a loan to get one because that would inflate the money supply too quickly and lead to a level of CPI inflation above their "target" level. So they will take actions to ensure that the interest rate is such that only a limited amount of money gets lent out. This results in there being a limited number from the line of potential borrowers that will want to take out loans.

The problem with this scenario is that the people wanting non-productive loans and the people wanting productive ones are all mixed in together. When a interest rate is chosen, and therefore a cut-off in the sorted line is made, there will be people who wanted productive loans who will have lost out to people who wanted non-productive ones. Had the line instead been sorted according to the loans of greatest benefit to society then there would have been a strong tendency for the productive loans to be ahead in the line.

To summarise the situation:

> **Non-productive loans lessen society's ability to lend for productive purposes.**

Investments and Pseudo-investments: Which do Banks Prefer?

Sadly politicians and economists around the world appear blissfully unaware of this fact. They certainly do almost nothing to suppress non-productive lending, which is especially sad because it would be relatively simple to address.

A very easy fix

All that would be required is a tax on non-productive loans. If someone is really so desperate to have that summer holiday without saving up for it first then they should pay compensation to the rest of society for the fact that they are hampering the progress of the nation's productivity.

Perhaps borrowing for non-productive purposes should be considered a social evil like smoking. Maybe advertising for such loans should be banned. Credit cards should be banned outright. All loans should be arranged person to person with bank managers – like the old days.

What you will see time and time again around the world is politicians proclaiming, "We must get interest rates lower so that we can have lots of investment." They may even add things like, "Yes, I know the lower interest rates will cause some inflation, but that's the price we have to pay for economic growth." If only they knew about all the harmful effects of non-productive loans. If we could discourage non-productive loans then with the same amount of total lending (i.e. have the same level of inflation) we could have more productive investments.

Counter-arguments (and their refutations)

Some free market fundamentalists are horrified when they hear suggestions of suppressing non-productive loans. They are liable to retort with several possible counter-arguments. We shall consider these in turn:

First, they may proclaim that a loan for consumption is beneficial to people other than the borrower. If the borrower wants to buy a new television, for example, then this will be of benefit to the television manufacturer. This is indeed true. We do not dispute this. The problem is with the *size* of the benefit. The benefit to the television manufacturer is in the *profit* it can make from the purchase of the television. The profit, however, is liable to be only a small fraction of the purchase price. So the benefit is small. Consider the following scenario: Imagine that you live in a town opposite a shirt-making factory. The factory uses inefficient machinery and its shirts are expensive. You like the design and quality but wish the shirts were cheaper. Let us say that a new, efficient shirt-making machine costs $5,000 and the factory owner would like to get one but doesn't have the money. One day a rich man comes to town with $5,000. Let's say that at this point one of two things could happen:

- The rich man buys $5,000 worth of shirts.

- The rich man lends the factory owner $5,000 to buy the new machine.

Which action is most likely to bring about cheaper shirts? We hope the answer is obvious.

Second, they may proclaim, "How dare you let some government bureaucrat decide who gets loans! That's communism!" This argument presupposes that we are suggesting that government bureaucrats are in charge of the entire loan selection process. This is not really the case.

A government bureaucrat would indeed need to draft a set of rules to define the most blatant forms of non-productive loans, thereby dividing all loan applications into two classes, but the choice about which loans are made within those classes would be made by the free market.

Third, they may claim that it is too difficult to distinguish between productive and non-productive loans. It is certainly true that with complex and creative accounting methods there may well be grey areas in this regard. But given the many harmful effects of lending for non-productive purposes, it is still beneficial to attempt to suppress clear-cut cases. To suggest otherwise is rather like suggesting that all crime should be allowed to go unpunished because there are some activities where it is not obvious whether they are criminal or not.

On a final note, please keep in mind that such widespread and ubiquitous borrowing for consumption (i.e. non-productive purposes) is a very modern invention. Discouraging it, is merely going back to how society has always worked in the past.

11 Pseudo-investment 1: Private Tailgating

The following few chapters will list some of the activities that the financial sector is involved in that have the aura of "investing" but upon closer inspection are simply pseudo-investments. But before we begin we need a little digression to introduce the concept of *financial tailgating*.

Financial tailgating

Tailgating to Glasgow

One of my pet annoyances while driving is tailgating. People insisting on driving too close to the car in front. I find it particularly irritating and stupid when on a long journey on a major road. I live in London, and Glasgow is a seven-hour journey along the M1 motorway. If someone tailgates me at the start of the journey I think to myself, "If this driver tailgates me all the way to Glasgow, they will get there about three seconds quicker than if they held back and left a reasonable distance between our cars." In a way, the tailgater has to pay a continuous penalty in terms of increased risk of an accident, both for them and for me, and for what? A journey that is 0.01% quicker? It hardly seems worth it. There appears to be an analogous phenomenon in economics which we will call *financial tailgating*.

Many people are so impatient to get their holiday, their car, their new furniture that they will forever be borrowing money to purchase these things. Not just as a one-off when they are very young, but throughout their lives. As soon as they've finished the repayments for one item they go out and borrow money for the next item. The benefit they get from this process is that they get their stuff earlier on in their lives but the penalty is having to pay a continuous stream of interest to banks.

Another way to appreciate the effect of tailgating is to compare the consumption patterns of two people born around the same time. Let's call them Tom and Simon. Tom is a compulsive tailgater. Simon always saves up until he has enough money before purchasing anything. There will be a period toward the start of their lives where the Tom the tailgater gets to have goods that Simon the saver does not have. Tom is "ahead" during this period. He gets to enjoy his goods while Simon has to endure a period of having less goods or perhaps putting up with poorer quality ones. Let's call this the "start-up" phase. After a while, when Simon has saved up some money and can start buying things, the situation becomes equalised: Both Tom and Simon can enjoy their ownership of the goods they want. This is a far longer period than the start-up. Call this the "post-start-up" phase. During the post start-up phase Tom is in a continuous state of paying a fraction of his income on interest to the banks. Simon has no such handicap and thus will be able to purchase slightly more or better quality goods than Tom for the rest of his life.

At this point it is important to highlight the difference between a financial tailgater and a true investor. Let us introduce a third character in our tale; let's call him Ivan the investor. Now before we continue, we need to consider their working lives. Tom, Simon and Ivan are all shoemakers. At the start of their working lives we already know that Tom borrowed money from the bank to buy new furniture and Simon simply started saving money toward new furniture later on, but Ivan the investor borrowed money from the bank to buy a new shoe-making machine that can make shoes in half the time. Now fast forward a few years. Simon is slightly ahead of Tom because he has now saved up enough to buy things like new furniture and does not have the burden of having to pay a continuous stream of interest to the banks. But Ivan is now ahead of both of them. He may still be having to pay interest to banks for the loan for the shoe-making machine, but having the machine has boosted his profitability so much that his increased income more than compensates for the interest repayments.

Hopefully this story should make it clear that tailgating is the *antithesis* of productive investing. Their outcomes are diametrically opposed. One results in a long-term *increase* in wealth, the other results in a long-term *decrease*. This fact makes it seem incredible how economists, politicians, the tax system and banking regulations often make very little effort to distinguish between the two phenomena. Remember also that banks in a free market do not distinguish between tailgating and productive investments because they only consider the interest repayments they can get on their loans. Banks have no incentive to consider what their loans are being used for. From the point of view of the banks, *all* loans are "investments" regardless of how the money is used.

Private tailgating

The first category we wish to list in this section on pseudo-investments is private tailgating: ordinary members of the public who are continuously buying things on credit, either through specific loans for major purchases or simply by virtue of having a credit card which they use on a regular basis. These people spend large chunks of their lives in a state of paying a continuous stream of interest to banks.

Mortgages

Loans to buy houses are clearly unproductive and therefore a pseudo-investment. Even if you agree with this statement you may be wondering how anyone could ever get to own their own homes if all pseudo-investments were discouraged. Well, home ownership and its cousin, land ownership, have some major problems which are not related to pseudo-investments, so we have placed a discussion of these in their own chapter later in the book.

12 Pseudo-investment 2: Government Tailgating

Because continuous tailgating is so short sighted and ultimately detrimental to your long-term wealth you might assume that governments would want no part of it, and yet they are regular offenders.

If you live in a country that is in a continuous state of being in debt, then your government is tailgating. The government may try to dress this up as a necessary "investment", but in reality most of the money will simply have been spent on the wages of government workers. Besides, if governments wanted to have more real investments in their economies then all they would have to do is discourage non-productive investments and this would release a tidal wave of money from savings that had previously been flowing into pseudo-investments.

The temptation for governments to tailgate is almost irresistible. The short-term benefits are just so convenient and the bad effects so subtle and, at least to start with, so far off in the future that country after country throughout history has become addicted to it, only to ultimately come unstuck.

A choice of mechanisms for making up tax shortfalls

Imagine for a moment a country with no national debt. An election is coming up and during the election a party promises to lower taxes. They go on to win, but once in power find that it is harder to cut back on government spending than they had anticipated. A government's spending is composed almost entirely of wages for government workers: police, firemen, teachers etc. So in order for governments to reduce their spending, they must either reduce the wages of their employees or reduce their number, both of which are likely to incur the wrath of unions or the electorate.

Printing the money

The easy cop-out for governments historically was often to simply print money to the tune of the shortfall in tax revenue. But printing more money often eventually brought about high inflation. Printing money like this brought about the collapse of so many currencies throughout history that this method became discredited. Indeed the very mention of the words "printing money" instantly brings about a strong mental picture of inflation in the minds of almost everyone, including most economists. Because of this fact, the idea of printing money as an economic device has become almost taboo. Many governments around the world have even enacted laws to ban the practice. The US, Japan and all the countries in the European Community all have such laws in place. This fact may sound strange to some readers because so many economics commentators have claimed that governments in these countries are in the process of printing money at the time of writing (2011). This claim is slightly misleading though, because what is actually happening is that governments are *borrowing* the money. Even if their central banks print (physically or electronically) fresh new money, the governments are not simply allowed to take that money and spend it. Instead they have to borrow it. We shall explain this odd mechanism in more detail later on in this chapter.

Borrowing the money from the private sector

The laws banning the practice of printing money have, however, left open the possibility of an alternative mechanism for making up tax shortfalls, namely borrowing the money. Borrowing the money comes in two flavours: borrowing from the private sector and borrowing from the central bank. It is important to consider these separately because they have rather different effects on the economy.

Borrowing *pre-existing* money from the private sector by issuing bonds is a rather special form of borrowing that does not increase the money supply like simple money printing would.

Bonds: What they are and how they work

At this point we need a short digression on the mechanism by which governments borrow money. They borrow via the process of issuing bonds. Bonds are a just a slightly more sophisticated IOU. They are a basic IOU with additional interest payments. So a government may just print up a piece of paper with something like the following written on it: "I promise to pay the owner of this bond $1 million in 10 years' time and additionally 3% interest each year". The government then offer these bonds for sale at $1 million each. Note that the interest paid each year (in this example 3%) is printed on the bond and will not change over the bond's lifespan. Also note that nobody in the private sector is compelled to purchase these bonds. Government bonds compete on the open market with all the other methods people have of earning interest on their money. If the interest rate offered on the bond is not enticing enough, then the bonds simply won't sell. Any prospective purchaser of a government bond will have to consider the following when determining whether a bond is worth purchasing:

1. The expected rate of inflation in the currency of the bond. This is critical because getting the $1 million back at the end of the term may not be much use if there has been massive inflation in the dollar and the purchasing power of that money has reduced.

2. The risk that the government will default on its repayment. This may seem like a very unlikely prospect, but it has happened on a pretty regular basis throughout history. If an investor considered that there was a 1% chance of a default, then they may demand an additional 1% extra in interest payments to compensate for this risk. This is known as the *risk premium*. Countries with a chequered financial history generally have to offer a higher rate of interest on their bonds than ones with a better reputation. There are even agencies that will award ratings (like AAA, BBB etc.) to governments according to their estimates of the chances of default, though in the wake of the sub-prime crisis these agencies themselves have now got a pretty poor reputation.

Finally the potential purchaser has to combine factors 1 and 2 and compare the resulting deal to all the other mechanisms available to them for gaining interest on their savings.

Some definitions: The interest paid on bonds is known as the *coupon*. The lifetime of the bond is called its *maturity* and the amount that has to be paid out at the end is called the *principal*. Confusingly, government bonds of different maturities get given different names like "T-bills", "Treasury notes" and "Treasury bonds" – but all you need to know is that they are all simply government bonds.

One of the additional reasons government tailgating through the process of continually issuing bonds is so attractive is that, superficially at least, it doesn't appear to cost anything. Interest payments on existing bonds can be paid for through the issuance of new bonds. So from the point of view of the government, the borrowing seems almost free.

The "penalty" incurred from government tailgating is in the form of a continuous flow of wealth from the nation as a whole to the holders of the bonds by way of interest payments.

Borrowing the money from the central bank

The alternative title for this subsection would be "A cheat and a fix (that doesn't work properly)"…

We must first point out that when a central bank purchases government bonds it does so by creating fresh new money. This means that borrowing from the central bank increases the money supply. When a government pays back the principal on the bonds, that money disappears out of existence, i.e. the money supply shrinks. The idea of a government owing money to its own central banks may sound a little odd. It's a bit like your left hand owing your right hand money! Indeed large fractions of the national debt for a wide range of countries are composed of debts to the countries own central banks. The reason for this odd state of affairs is all to do with the governments stated legal commitment that they will not simply "print money" to make up tax shortfalls.

A devious trick…

As already mentioned, many countries have made it illegal for governments to simply print money in times of need. But presented with the information that a government is allowed to *borrow* money from its central bank, a sneaky politician may hatch the following plan: The government could print up a load of bonds offering zero interest then instruct their central bank to purchase them. The central bank would do this by printing up fresh new money and handing that over to the government. When the bonds mature and it is time to pay back the principal, the governments could just repeat the process indefinitely. This would just be a devious way of effectively printing fresh new money to cover tax shortfalls.

The rule to prevent the trick

To prevent this trick there are rules stating that central banks are not allowed to purchase bonds *directly* from their governments. Instead governments are required to sell the bonds on the open market, forcing them to offer a competitive interest rate, and then the central banks are allowed to buy the bonds back from the market. This may all seem a little convoluted, but it is simply a mechanism to ensure that whenever a government borrows from its central bank a proper "market" rate of interest is paid.

Problems with the rule

The problem with this rule is that the "market" rate of interest can become distorted. If there is a sustained period in which central banks are buying up large quantities of government bonds then the market will become aware of this fact. It may lead to a situation in which a major reason that the market will purchase the bonds is because it knows that there are ready buyers. This artificially keeps the interest rate that needs to be offered on the bonds lower than it would be otherwise. A super-low interest rate on new borrowing serves only to entice governments to borrow ever larger sums.

This is now a dangerous game, a slippery slope. It can work for a substantial period, allowing government debt to rise to extraordinary highs, but at some point the "market" will become nervous about whether the government can carry on doing this forever. If they fear that the central bank may stop buying the ever growing stream of new bonds then they would need a higher interest payment to be offered on the bonds to entice them to purchase. This quickly instigates a positive feedback mechanism in which the rising interest rates make it even less likely that the government can continue to borrow. This in turn means that an even higher level of interest needs to be offered.

Eventually the government won't be able to sell new bonds at all. Their borrowing ability will simply cease. The tax shortfall will likely be enormous at this point, and without new borrowing large numbers of government workers will have to be laid off. Unemployment will skyrocket. What happens next depends on too many variables to cover in this book but it will invariably be pretty ugly and may well involve civil unrest.

Avoiding the disaster scenario (is very hard to do)

To avoid the slippery slope scenario a government would need to reduce the amount of bonds purchased by its central bank and even put the process in reverse, i.e. have taxes high enough so that there is an excess of funds. This excess can then be used to pay down the principal on all the bonds held by its central bank. Remember that when the government pays back the principal to its central bank the money expires and the money supply shrinks.

This process is doubly tortuous for any government. First of all it will have to be brave enough to tax more than it's spending. It is usually a pretty tough job to get elected on a platform of higher taxes and lower spending. Don't forget that lower spending invariably means putting government workers out of a job. Second, the money supply is going to be falling throughout the process. This causes pain for mortgage holders who will find it increasingly difficult to make their mortgage payments. Add in a little paradox of thrift type unemployment and you have a recipe for such an uncomfortable situation that governments will simply be incapable of carrying it out.

There was probably never any need for government borrowing in the first place!

Politicians that propose government borrowing will invariably insist that the money is essential for investment. At first glance this may sound like a reasonable proposition. The idea that government borrowing may serve as a good investment relies on drawing an analogy between the country as a whole and a small business, but this analogy is flawed. A country is in fact more like a super-large business and there is a key difference in how it behaves in terms of investment strategies:

The difference between a small company and a big one

Imagine a small business that makes shoes. The workers are highly expert in all aspects of leather, rubber, glue, thread etc. They want a new machine that will help produce shoes more efficiently. It would generally be completely impractical and highly inefficient for the workers in that company to attempt to build that new machine themselves. Building machines that make shoes is a very different thing to the process of making the shoes themselves. The expertise required in metal working, electronics, motors etc. is a completely different skill set. It makes much more sense for the company to borrow the money for the new machine. There is, of course, a penalty in terms of interest to be paid, but the company has no reasonable choice.

Now consider the investment behaviour of a super-large company. When we say super-large, we don't mean just a large shoe-making company, we mean one of those *huge* do-it-all companies like Samsung or Mitsubishi, the kind of company that makes everything from chewing gum to supertankers. If one of these companies had a shoe-making division and a machine tool division then when the shoe-making division wanted a new machine to make shoes more efficiently it would make more sense for the higher management to simply ask one division to build the machine for the other. There is no need at all for any loans, and no need to be paying any interest on this investment.

A country is far more analogous to the super-large company. Most, if not all the investment functions can be performed internally. If you want to have more investment, then simply assign more people to the divisions which produce machine tools.

The analogy between a country and a super-large company is not perfect; after all, in the case of a country the "shoe-making division" and the "machine tools division" are most likely different companies, but the essential feature remains – a country can have perfectly adequate levels of investment *internally*. Higher levels of investment in a country simply equate to a higher proportion of the workforce carrying out "investment" type work. In general, a government does not have to go into debt at all in order to have investment going on within its economy.

Even if businesses in an under-developed country cannot source machine tools from within their country, there is still no reason for *government* borrowing. If it makes sense for a business within that country to borrow to buy new machinery, then there is no reason at all that the company cannot borrow directly from a bank. There is no need for any government involvement.

13 Pseudo-investment 3: (Most) Share Dealing

People may be surprised at seeing share dealing listed under the heading of pseudo-investments. There is a general perception that trading stocks and shares is simply an indirect mechanism for investing in companies. However, more than 99% of share dealing transactions give no benefit whatsoever to the company whose shares are being traded. It is true that when a company issues shares and they are purchased in the first instance (a so-called *Initial Public Offering* or IPO) the money paid goes directly to the company and so may be used for productive investment. However, if and when company shares get sold on in the so-called *secondary market*, possibly a great many times, *none* of the subsequent selling price goes to the company, even if the price of the shares soars.

Many people argue that the fact that shares are allowed to be sold on and traded means that the initial purchasers (the people who buy the IPOs) will be willing to pay a higher price than would be the case if subsequent trades were discouraged or not allowed. Therefore, they argue, a free and enthusiastic secondary share-dealing market is an essential part of investing in business. In this chapter we will argue that this claim, while true, is rather overstating the case. There are indeed some advantages of having a secondary market in shares, but allowing this market to be entirely unrestricted leads to some truly awful consequences which have been overlooked by most economists. In this section we intend to show that the benefits of an entirely unrestricted secondary market are small and the problems caused are very large indeed.

Initial share sales (this is the good bit that works)

At the most fundamental level, the reason people buy shares is for the collection of dividend payments. If an individual or a bank has some cash they want to invest and earn money with, they can examine the prospectuses of the latest companies that are in the process of issuing shares and choose one or more which they believe will become profitable and be able to pay high dividends. This is true investment, the way it is supposed to be: Skilled investors, able to spot a good business plan, guiding resources toward companies that are most likely to prosper. These kinds of investors are performing a function that is of great benefit to society. The more skilled they are, the better society's resources will be guided. There will be less wasted effort on poorly thought out business plans. If these investors get it right then the rewards will be great, both for the investors themselves and for society as a whole. If one of the companies they have shares in starts making good profits then the investors will start collecting large dividend payments.

A company can only be successful if it's making something that people want, either something that was previously unavailable or perhaps something that is better or cheaper than the existing competition. This is a win-win situation for the shareholders and the public. The free market is working. Adam Smith's "invisible hand" is doing its job perfectly. The selfish acts of the investors for their

156

own personal reward serve to benefit society as a whole through new, better or cheaper goods.

Unrestricted secondary share dealing and price accuracy?

It is very likely that some people reading this will be thinking that the assumption that people should buy shares for dividend payments is wrong. They will point out that many people buy shares largely because they think the price of the shares will rise. They think that the profit they can make from a rising share price is more significant than any dividend payments that they could get from owning shares for a short period. In this section we will examine the practice of buying and selling shares over short periods with an aim to making money primarily from changes in the price rather than from dividend payments.

If you were considering whether or not to buy some shares and hold on to them forever and benefit purely from dividend payments then you have some obvious business-related problems to solve, i.e. what is your expectation of future dividends and does the price of the shares represent good value for this future income stream. This will depend on how well run the company is, the size of the potential market for the company's products, what its competition is like etc. etc. One thing you *don't* have to think about is how valuable *other* share traders think the shares are. If you are correct in your estimate of future dividend payments and you think the shares represent good value while the other traders incorrectly think that future dividend payments will be poor, then you can just snap up the bargain shares and then later sit on your deckchair on the beach sipping Martinis and enjoy your large dividend payments forever more. You can occasionally have a chuckle to yourself about how wrong everyone else was.

> **If you are going to hold on to shares forever then the only things you need to consider are the price and your estimate of future dividend payments. You do not need to consider the opinions of other share dealers.**

Contrast this share purchase decision to that when your plan is to only own shares for a short period. Suddenly the opinion of everyone else becomes critical. To see why this is so, consider the following tale:

Short-term share dealing

Imagine a dealer called Harry. He has been instructed to buy and sell company shares within one working day and maximise his profit. This scenario is actually so commonly practised that it even has its own name: *day trading*. Let's consider what Harry needs to think about in order to maximise his profits. Let's say for a moment that Harry is super-expert in business plans and company valuations. It's his first day on the job. He (perhaps naively) assumes that what he needs to do is find shares that are cheap, buy them in the morning, then sell them in the evening when their price may have risen a small fraction. Harry starts some laborious, painstaking research and according to his calculations of expected future dividend payments shares in Company X should be worth $10 each. But Harry notes that they have been trading steadily at around $12 for months. What is he to think? Is it him who's wrong or is it the other market participants?

Let's say for a moment that he concludes that he is right and its everyone else who's wrong, either because he thinks that he is smarter than the average trader, or perhaps because he can see an explanation for a share to be overpriced that he suspects other people have not taken into consideration – something about

Company X that looks superficially good but, when analysed more carefully or with Harry's specialist expertise, is not so exciting after all. Harry may consider that, assuming that he is right, in the very long term the existing share owners will see that the dividend payments (which are generally infrequent) are on the small side considering the price of the shares. They will eventually see that the shares represent a poor return on investment. So he may say to himself that the long-term outlook for the price of those shares is negative, though the downward correction to the share price might only occur many months or even years into the future. There is always that tiny risk that the downward correction could happen during that day so he feels generally disinclined to buy these shares.

So far his investigations have come to nothing: He has not found a good money-making opportunity.

The early news trick
Suddenly the phone rings. On the other end of the line is his trusted friend Bob. Bob mixes in high circles and is usually among the first to know about all sorts of political and high finance gossip. Bob tells Harry that he thinks there is going to be some changes in the tax system which will have an impact on Company X. It's an easy calculation to see that Company X will be able to make 1% greater profits than before and so the true value of its shares will rise (by *his* calculations) from to $10.00 to $10.10 per share. Bob also knows that the official news about the new regulations will be broadcast at lunchtime and everyone in the market will find out about it then.

What should Harry do with this information? His initial thought is that even with an expected future dividend stream that is 1% higher, the stock will *still* be poor value if trading at $12. So its long-term outlook is *still* negative and he should still not buy shares in Company X. But then if he thinks a little bit longer... he may realise that even though *he* thinks that the rest of the market is overvaluing the share, if $12 is the price that *they* are thinking is reasonable, they are almost certain to raise their estimates of the value after the lunchtime news. Certainly the chances of the price going up after the news is way higher than the chances that the price will go down despite the fact that Harry thinks it is generally overpriced; after all, the market has already shown that it considers $12 to be reasonable. Harry has a clear opportunity to make a profit by buying some shares before the news and selling them again when the price has gone up in the afternoon. For convenience, let's label this idea the "early news trick". From Harry's point of view this makes perfect sense. Even though he thinks the rest of the market has overvalued the stock, it is still perfectly logical for him to buy the shares and sell them later in the day for a small profit.

Let us summarise what has just happened:

> **An intelligent person may decide to buy shares at a price which they themselves think is too high. This has not been caused by some temporary irrationality but by perfectly sound logic.**

Notice that this trick is only an option in a system where there is no restriction on secondary trades. If there was a small tax penalty on secondary trades where the stock is owned for too short a period then this trick would not work. The tax penalty would destroy this profit-making opportunity. But also note that carrying out the trick would not have benefited Company X in any way, so the absence of the opportunity to perform this trick does not constitute a loss to Company X. The consequences of the trick would simply have been a transfer of wealth from a trader who got news late or was only able to respond to it slowly to a trader who got the news early and was able to respond to it quickly.

At this point some people may say that the early news trick is a fantasy, or very rare. It may constitute insider trading (which is illegal), or they may point out that government regulatory changes are kept perfectly secret until they are announced publicly to everyone at the same time. In response to this we would say that they were probably being naive, and besides, there is ample scope for employing the early news trick without insider trading or advance notice of government announcements. For example, you may hear some news being announced at the same time as everyone else but simply react quicker than the other traders. It may be that it is actually quite tricky to work out the consequences of the news report for the value of Company X. If you can work out the consequences in five seconds while it takes your rivals ten seconds to work it out, then you win: You can do the early news trick. This is precisely why you so often see panicked-looking traders shouting down telephones trying to buy or sell as fast as possible when important news breaks. Every second counts; even fractions of a second could be important.

Note: From this point on, when we use the word "news" it does not necessarily mean "world events" type news, it could just be some financial figures being made public.

Some may argue that even though the availability of the early news trick has no impact on the money that actually goes to Company X in the first place it is still of benefit to anyone whose pension or savings are being managed by Harry. It should be pointed out, however, that any money that Harry earns through the early news trick is always at the cost of another trader who is looking after *someone else*'s savings or pension. So there is no net benefit of Harry's speedy response to the economy as a whole.

So far we have seen that the availability of the early news trick is perhaps of no benefit to the economy. Now let's consider any potential *harm* the practice could do. In order to do this, let us go back to Harry and consider his thought processes again...

In the beginning of the story we told you that Harry had laboriously and painstakingly researched and calculated the true value of the Company X only to decide that it was a poor buy. But after getting that phone call from Bob and working out that he could do the early news trick, he should have realised that he need not have gone to all that trouble. The fact that he disagreed with the evaluation that the rest of the market had given Company X did not matter! This is a crucial realisation:

> In order to profit from short-term share trades, you only need to consider likely *changes* to a share price from its current market valuation caused by immediate news and events. It is generally* of little consequence whether you happen to disagree with the current evaluation as determined by the rest of the market.
>
> *The word "generally" is here because under certain circumstances it can indeed become important, but we shall get to that later.

Before we go on to discuss the consequences of this realisation we need to consider the existence of two phenomena: noise and market errors.

Noise and market errors

Noise
The word "noise" is used in a wide variety of mathematical and technical fields. It can be thought of as a kind of small jitter or disturbance. Shares that are subject to frequent buying and selling will be subject to noise in their price.

Imagine for a second that there is no interesting news at the moment about Company Y. Imagine also that over the next hour 100 people will buy shares in Company Y and correspondingly 100 people will sell. When each individual share trade is made, it may affect the price a tiny amount. In keeping with the principle of supply and demand discussed earlier, a sale of a share acts as a signal that the price should come down a tiny amount, whereas the purchasing of a share acts as a signal that the price should go up. The person instigating the trade is the one who sends the signal.

So now let us consider the 100 share trades that are due to happen in the next hour. Imagine that in 50 of the trades the seller announces his intention to sell and the buyer simply responds by purchasing, and in the other 50 the buyer announces his desire to buy and the seller simply responds to that offer. The net effect on the selling price after all the trades should be zero.

But now let's consider the order in which these sales take place. Assuming they occur randomly, it is most unlikely that the market will get signals in a neat order: buy... sell... buy... sell... It is much more likely that the signals will come in disorderly clumps, with two or three sell signals in succession followed by several buy signals. This means that the price of the shares will jitter up and down by small amounts purely at random. The jitters do not correspond to any news or analysis, but are simply random. |

> **Market errors**
>
> People make mistakes. Even the smartest of people forget things, they can have gaps in their knowledge, they can make errors in their maths, they can get ideas conflated, they can be hungover from the night before... If they are in charge of purchasing large amounts of shares for a big bank they can make a mistake that will alter the share price slightly. If they *buy* shares due to a mistake then they will push the share price up. If they *sell* shares due to a mistake then they will push the price down. All for no fundamentally good reason. Let's label this phenomenon a *market error*.
>
> These errors will no doubt happen on a daily basis. There will also be much smaller players in the market, with much less expertise, buying and selling smaller quantities of shares. The likelihood of them doing so for unsound reasons is far higher, though the effect their actions will have on the share price will be smaller. Those kinds of errors may happen many times per day, probably even many times per minute!

Noise and market errors will combine to make share prices jitter up and down for reasons that are nothing at all to do with the fundamentals of the true value of the shares. They are just a kind of "junk" signal that gets mixed in with the well-considered trades made by experts that are on top form and not hungover or otherwise below par. You may assume that this junk component of the signal is harmless, and the market will somehow cope with it in some rational way... but hold on. We have a problem. Most trades in the stock market are to own shares for short periods which means that the price of the shares is determined by the buying and selling activities of people employing the early news trick. These people have little incentive to accurately calculate the true value of shares based on fundamentals. Their modus operandi is to assume that the current price is somehow "correct" or "the well-considered valuation of the rest of the market" and all they need think about is the possible *change* to that price caused by the latest news.

Imagine that at some point the price of Company X rose by 0.5%. What should Harry think? Is it noise? Is it a market error? Is it the new, well-considered opinion by the rest of the market caused by some events that Harry is unaware of, or that Harry is aware of but is unaware has any impact on the value of Company X? He has no way of telling, and what's more, the other market participants have no way of telling either! There is no obvious action Harry can take in response to this 0.5% change. He may as well take no action at all and simply keep tuned to the news and hope for another handy phone call from Bob.

In a market where most participants are employing the early news trick, there is no good mechanism for correcting noise and market errors.

The consequence of this is that at any one time the price will correspond to the sum of a series of small changes which are either noise, market errors or quick reactions to news events as they happen. This is a perfect recipe for the share price to drift away from its logical market value based purely on expected future dividends.

Considering the knowledge of other share dealers

Let's re-join the story of Harry the day trader. It's now the start of day two on the job. Harry is delighted with himself for having discovered the early news trick and has made a nice profit from having purchased shares in Company X before lunch and selling them in the afternoon. Suddenly the phone rings. It's Bob again. This time the gossip from Bob is slightly different. Bob has just been tipped off by some pollsters that the election results in

Maltovia are set to be a surprise victory for the left-wing party, overturning years of rule by the right wing. The result of the election is going to be announced at lunchtime.

Harry takes a moment to digest this information. He tries to work out if there is any impact of the election result on the future profitability of Company X. This time the connection is not nearly as obvious as the tax change. There are two factors to consider.

First of all the left-wing government is going to impose a 10% import tariff on foreign goods. This will clearly have a negative effect on the future profitability of Company X because it will sell fewer of it products to that country. Everyone knows this fact as it was trailed as the flagship policy of the left-wing party.

But Harry, who is a very smart guy, happens to also know some much less well publicised information: He knows that the left-wing government wants to impose strict new environmental controls on its mining companies which will dramatically push up the price of Maltovia's main export: neutronium. Harry knows that neutronium is an important constituent of a product that is a rival to that produced by Company X. So a rise in costs for Company X's rivals is clearly good news for Company X. Harry realises that, because the population of Maltovia is so small, the reduction in sales due to the import tariff will be more than compensated for by the much larger positive effect of the higher priced neutronium.

Harry calculates that the net effect of the two factors combined on the future dividend payments is a small increase of around perhaps 5%. Harry is correct in his calculations.

We now want to consider whether Harry can use this information to do the early news trick again. Now he has a real conundrum. The problem is that the connection between the election result and the change in the value of the company is much harder to deduce. Some people may not know that the rival product relies on neutronium, some people may not know that it is the intention of the new left-wing government to introduce the new environmental controls, but everyone knows about the import duty. Harry thinks to himself that if the market is dominated by people who only know about the import duty then the price of the shares will go down after the results are announced, but if most people also know about the environmental controls and the composition of the rival products then the price will go up. The likelihood of the early news trick working is now critically dependent on the knowledge and intelligence of the other market participants, and Harry knows it.

At this point let us consider the evolution of Harry's job:

> **Harry started out on day one thinking that his job was to accurately estimate the value of shares based on expected future dividend payments.**

But then came Bob's first phone call which alerted Harry to the early news trick.

> **Harry could virtually ignore his own estimate of the value of shares and simply consider his estimate of *changes* to the value of shares based on news events.**

But then came Bob's second phone call which alerted Harry to the need to consider other people's knowledge and intelligence.

> **Harry now realises that he has to estimate other people's estimate of how the news will change share prices.**

And now it gets worse still. Harry thinks some more and realises that the other market participants will all be playing the same game. There may be other people out there who are smart enough to know that the price should rise but are assuming that most *other* market participants are not so smart, so they may bet on a fall despite knowing that the effect of the news is positive for Company X. It's rather like being at the cinema and noticing a very subtle gag, perhaps a certain facial expression, a raising of an eyebrow… You may chuckle to yourself, smugly thinking that you're the only one in the cinema who got the joke... Little do you realise that the entire cinema is full of people smugly thinking they are the only ones who got the joke.

> **Harry now realises he has to estimate other people's estimates of other people's estimates of how the news will change share prices!**

Harry has come a long way from his ideas at the start of day one.

No less a figure than John Maynard Keynes had deduced many of these features of stock market pricing back in 1936 in his book *The General Theory of Employment Interest and Money*. One feature in particular, the idea of investors predicting what other investors are thinking, has even been given the label: *a Keynesian beauty contest*.

So now we can see that the evolution of the share price of Company X is looking truly mangled. As the months and years go by, its price will end up as the sum of a collection of changes, each of which are based on noise and market errors that don't efficiently get corrected, and a collection of short-term reactions to news by people who are aiming to predict how other people predict how other people will predict changes in the price. This process is a perfect recipe for *compounding errors*. It's rather analogous to the following scenario:

Imagine there is a big jar of coins collected from around the world. No two coins are alike. You are set the task of answering the following question: If all the coins were to be balanced one on top of the other, how tall would the stack be? You have a choice of two methods to work this out. Method one is to simply make the stack and then measure it. Method two is to separately measure the thickness of each coin and then add up all the thicknesses. Hopefully it is obvious to you that method one is likely to be more accurate. What's more it should also be obvious that the greater the number of coins, the larger the error of method two is likely to be. Given the fact that bulk of share trading is carried out over very short periods, the share prices are largely determined in a way analogous to method two.

At this point we could go on to describe Bob's phone calls on days three, four and five which will give Harry even more ideas about how to profit from his day trading. With each phone call, Harry will realise more and more things that he needs to consider that have less and less relation to estimating the likely future dividend payments of Company X and more and more to do with the psychology and behaviour of other market participants. But we will spare you the gory details. You should be getting the idea by now:

> **Share prices can easily drift a long way from a value that corresponds to anyone's estimate of future dividend payments.**

Fisher Black, an economist made famous for his contribution to the "Black-Scholes equation", once suggested that the market was doing well if the price of shares was within a factor of two (i.e. between double and half) of its true value. In a talk he gave in 1986 he said: "The factor of 2 is arbitrary, of course. Intuitively though, it seems reasonable to me, in the light of sources of uncertainty about value and the strength of the forces tending to cause price to return to value."

What is the benefit of unrestricted secondary share dealing?

So now we have seen that the effect of unrestricted secondary share dealing is wildly varying and "irrational" prices. This is clearly a big minus to any economy. The question we wish to address now is: Was it worth it? Is the upside of allowing unrestricted share dealing so large that it is worth enduring some crazy share evaluations?

The argument goes that allowing unrestricted secondary shares means that a company can sell at a higher price at its IPO, but is it a large amount more? A small amount? Something in between? Obviously it will depend on exactly what type of restriction is placed on secondary share trades. Let's try a thought experiment to investigate this issue...

Imagine a company director, let's call him Fred. He wants to sell all or part of his company for some reason; perhaps he needs the money for new machinery or perhaps he wants to sell up in order to start a new business altogether. He declares to the market that he is going to issue shares for sale for the first time. He hires a big hall and invites a large collection of potential purchasers (this isn't how it's done in practice, of course, this is just a thought experiment). He gets up on a stage at the front of the hall and makes an announcement: "My company is well run and profitable. Please buy my shares and you shall receive high dividend payments for years to come." The people have been given prospectuses with all the business plans, forecasts, the latest accounts etc. They have had ample opportunity to determine just how good a purchase the shares will be.

Now imagine each person in the room has been given a special device with a keypad and they are instructed to secretly type in the highest price they would be willing to pay for the shares and how many shares they would buy at that price. A computer connected to all these devices would then work out the optimal selling price such that the company earned the greatest amount of money from the sale. The people in the room busily type in their numbers. The computer does its calculations and declares that Fred should offer his shares at exactly $100 each. The computer has worked out that $100 is the highest price he could charge such that all the shares get sold. Any more and some would go unsold; any less and there would be disappointed customers that would be unable to purchase. The price of $100 will exactly balance supply and demand for the shares.

An important digression on the $100 selling price

Note that the people who end up without shares are not doing so because they offered zero or made no bid at all. There would probably be many people who simply bid too little. Assuming the pool of potential customers was large then there would probably be plenty of people who typed in a bid just short of $100, say perhaps $99.50 or $99...

Fred is just about to instigate the procedure to actually make the sale, but before he has time to press the metaphorical "sell now" button, he gets interrupted... It just so happens that there is a radio on in the corner of the hall, and just at that moment a newsreader says, "The Ministry of Finance has just made a surprise new law about share dealing. Anyone who buys shares, either an initial share issue or a secondary trade, is to be discouraged from re-selling them within a period of less than one month. Anyone re-selling within a shorter period will have to pay a penalty tax of 2%."

The people in the hall take a few minutes to digest this news and consider its impact. They demand that Fred cancel the current bids and redo the auction. Fred makes an announcement: "Please now adjust the figures you previously typed into your devices, taking into account the news we have just heard."

The question is, what will this new, post-announcement price be? Will it still be $100? Will it drop to $98? $90? $0?

In order to answer this question we need to consider the plans and motivations of the people in the room. If someone fully intends to invest in the company for many years to come, then pretty much *any* type of restriction on reselling the shares is going to be of very little or no consequence. If it is someone's firm intention from the outset to only hold on to the shares for ten minutes, then their plans will be ruined by the announcement. They may conceivably drop their bid to zero. But now we need to ask – why would someone want to buy shares and then sell them ten minutes later?

The only conceivable reason someone would want, from the outset, to own shares for some very short period is if they personally knew *in advance* of some information that would only become apparent to the rest of the market *during* that short period. If that information was already known to the market before the sale then that information would already be factored in to the price and no conceivable advantage could be gained. Similarly if that information was to become available only *after* the short period, then again no advantage can be gained. The shorter the period in question, the less likely it is that any of the bidders knows a) such a piece of information and b) that the information is likely to become apparent to the rest of the market during that short period.

Some people may say, "Okay, but what if someone has no particular plan (at the outset) to sell after only a short period, but they would like the flexibility to freely sell at *any* time because they may suddenly and unexpectedly need to use their savings?" Indeed there may be many people in that position. You may then assume that these people would then lower their bid in order to compensate for the *possibility* that they may have to pay the penalty tax. Note that this is a possibility rather than a certainty, and this is crucial. If someone thought that the probability of having to sell their shares within one month was 10%, then the amount by which they would drop their offer would *not* be the full value of the penalty tax, but something in the order of 10% of that amount, i.e. 0.2%.

Some people may say, "Okay, but what if someone has no particular plan (at the outset) to sell after only a short period but they would like the flexibility to freely sell at any time so that they can quickly sell if the share price falls?" This is a more complicated issue. We now need to consider things like the potential share purchaser's perception of the probability of a sudden fall, along with an estimate of the size of any falls and also the probability that the purchaser can *anticipate* the fall. After all, if there is a sudden fall and you are too slow to react and are still owning the shares after the fall has occurred then there is little point selling now. The damage has already been done. The new lower price should now, in theory, be set so that it once again corresponds to the current value of predicted future earnings. So if you don't think you can anticipate a sudden fall then you have no reason at all to lower your original bid. Even if you do think you can anticipate a fall then the most you could lose through having to sell in a hurry is the 2% penalty.

Taking all these factors into consideration, the drop in the price that Fred would suffer due to the 2% penalty is likely to be *less* than 2%, because some fraction of the people will no doubt perceive that the probability that they will be forced to sell during the one month period is low or even zero.

We could have described the share sale thought experiment with a variety of different announcements being broadcast on the radio about different types of restrictions on secondary share trades, different sized penalties, different minimum ownership periods or entirely different types of restrictions, and in each case there would be different corresponding reductions in the post-announcement price compared to the original.

In Table 13-1 we have drawn up some, admittedly unscientific, estimates of the relationships between different announcements and the size of the effect on the original selling price. We do not claim that these figures are necessarily accurate or that they are based on any empirical evidence. We merely suggest that a) they are a reasonable guess and b) it is reasonable to assume that small restrictions on secondary share trading would have only a very minor effect on the amount of true investment (i.e. the money that goes to the original company) that is achieved through the entirety of the share purchasing and trading system.

Restriction on secondary share trades	Guesstimated fraction of unrestricted initial selling price
5% tax on all secondary share trades if selling within one year of purchase	96%
4% tax on all secondary share trades if selling within one month of purchase	97%
3% tax on all secondary share trades if selling within one week of purchase	99%
2% tax on all secondary share trades if selling within one hour of purchase	99.9%

Table 13-1 How restrictions on short-term share dealing may affect investment.

The new wave paradox

To illustrate some of the problems caused when people are purchasing shares, planning to make money from changes in the price rather than dividend payments, we shall examine an effect we shall call the "new wave paradox". This is a scenario in which a new wave of investors, or alternatively a set of investors putting new money into the stock market, foolishly thinks that their purchases are doing particularly well while in fact they are becoming steadily poorer value. In order to fully understand this effect we need a model of the share dealing system as a whole. In particular we need to look at the inflows and outflows of money.

Harking back to the chapter on supply and demand, a good way to visualise these flows is to consider an analogy with a container with liquid flowing into it from the top and liquid flowing out of the bottom. We shall now develop this model with a few added details specific to the stock market. See Figure 13-1.

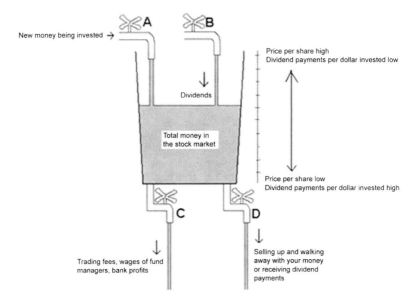

Figure 13-1 A visualisation of share prices.

As you can see there are only two possible sources of money for the entire system:

- New money that was not previously tied up in the stock market being used to buy shares, either primary or secondary share purchases.

- Dividend payments being used to purchase more shares.

There are two possible mechanisms for money being taken out of the system:

- The fees/profits/wages etc. of the people who are employed to run the system.

- The dividend payments and/or payments from others when you sell your shares and take your money out of the system altogether.

One flow of money we have deliberately chosen not to show is money flowing inside the system. This flow can happen when a trader sells shares in one company, only to immediately (or within a short period) buy shares in another. These internal flows are of no consequence in the explanations that follow.

Now that the model is set up we can begin to explore some interesting characteristics of the system.

The first thing to notice is that the total value of all the shares in a stock market can change in a way that depends on the relative rates of flow into and out of it. If the rates of flow were balanced then the value of the shares would remain at a constant level. If for some reason there was a period in which new money was entering the system at a slower rate than the aforementioned equilibrium level then the price of the shares would fall. Conversely if for some reason there was a period in which new money was entering the system at a faster rate than the equilibrium level then the price of the shares would rise. If shares become more expensive while the dividend stream remained constant then this would mean that the dividends paid per dollar of money invested would go down. Another way of saying this is as follows:

> **All else being equal, the more money there is invested in the stock market, the less each dollar invested will earn in terms of dividend payments.**

It's a bit like saying that the more animals go to a small stream to drink, the less water each one can receive.

Now that we have deduced this relationship, we can now answer the question of how much money *should* be invested in the stock market. The answer, perhaps oddly, actually depends on the rates of return available in *rival* investment schemes (of similar perceived risk).

To see why, imagine for a moment that an alternative investment type, let's call it System X, were averaging 5% returns. Imagine also that the dividend payments on the stock market were averaging only 3% returns on the money invested. Clearly System X is a better place to put your money. What should happen now is that people start abandoning the stock market in favour of System X. As you can deduce from the diagram, this extra flow out of Tap D will lessen the price of shares. This ties in with the supply and demand mechanism, i.e. extra selling will act as a signal that prices should fall. Shares having a lower price will mean that the dividend payments per dollar invested in shares go up. This outflow from the stock market would continue until the dividend payments per dollar invested rose to 5%.

Conversely if the stock market was earning investors more than System X, say 8% in dividends per dollar invested, then the opposite would happen: People would see that the stock market was better than System X and start rushing into the stock market. This would correspond to extra fast flow at Tap A. This would cause the price of shares to rise and correspondingly the dividend payments per dollar invested to fall. Again this would continue until the rate of return, i.e. dividend payments per dollar invested, fell to 5%.

To summarise:

> **The total investment in the stock market *should* be continually adjusting itself such that its returns per dollar invested are approximately the same as rival investment systems.***
>
> * In practice this may not happen for a reasons you shall soon see.

We are now ready to introduce the new wave paradox:

Imagine that during some period of time, the stock market was approximately in equilibrium, i.e. in Figure 13-1 A + B is

178

approximately equal to C + D and so share prices are roughly steady. Now imagine that for some reason there was a wave of new money entering the stock market over and above the equilibrium level. How would the system respond?

We have already shown that what *should* happen is that as the dividends per dollar invested starts to fall there will be a greater tendency for other market participants to sell up and invest in something other than stocks. But, as discussed earlier in this chapter, all those day traders are generally paying little attention to the absolute value of the dividend payments per share (within reason). They will not be in any rush to leave the stock market just because the start of a wave of new money caused the share prices to rise by a few per cent.

The people at the start of the new wave will think that what they've done has been a great success. They will be saying to themselves, "Look, the price of my shares have risen. If I sold them I'd have a tidy profit. I'm so smart!" This is a paradox because normally the price of something should rise only if it becomes *more* valuable. Certainly if there was no new wave then the only way an *individual* company's share price could rise is if there was some new evidence that its future dividend payments would be *higher* than previously expected. But what we're observing here, with the new wave, is the price of shares rising while the value of future dividend payments per dollar invested is falling... and everybody seems happy with the result!

This paradox is very deceiving and very damaging as we shall see...

After the initial success of the new wave of investors, they may tell their friends what a great thing the stock market is. The likely future dividends per dollar invested will have gone down slightly, but in the eyes of those involved in the new wave that won't matter a jot because the price of their shares has risen nicely. The friends of the "new wavers" may want to get some of that action and they may add new money to the system. They will soon be saying, "Gee, this stock market stuff is great. The dividends are a bit small, but I will make a fortune because the price of my shares is rising. When I sell, I'll be rich."

Even more money will start entering the system. Prices of shares will go up. Dividend payments per dollar invested will go down...

People will then start saying, "Gee, the dividend payments are tiny, but who cares when the prices are rising so nicely." People may start borrowing (= creating) money to invest in the stock market because the prices are rising so fast.

Notice that at this point there will be many people *thinking* that they have great wealth. The value of their investments has risen sky high. But also notice that they are not yet rich, because they have not yet actually got their money. At the moment they are just rich *in theory*. Converting theory into practice involves actually selling your shares...

Trouble is brewing. The smarter investors will start thinking to themselves, "These guys are nuts. They're paying higher and higher prices for shares whose inherent value (i.e. dividend payments per dollar invested) is getting less and less. This can't go on forever. I think I'd better exit the stock market altogether before it all collapses." The people who are first to have this realisation will be fine. They will convert their high price shares into cash and walk away. Tap D is beginning to open a bit wider...

If the amount of money in the stock market is particularly large then another type of trouble may also be brewing. Notice that there may have been some extended period in which more and more people have invested in the stock market and/or more and more money may have been borrowed in order to invest. There is a natural limit on just how many new investments (Tap A) there can be. Maybe everyone who *could* conceivably have invested *has already* invested. Maybe everyone who was tempted to borrow in order to invest has already borrowed the maximum anyone would allow them to. Maybe sources of new money entering the system are beginning to simply run out. This will mean that there is no possibility that prices can rise any higher... and if the only reason people were excited about entering the stock market was because of share price rises then the excitement will start to disappear. The price chart will start to flatten. The *remaining* reason to own shares, i.e. dividend payments, will now correspond to a very poor rate of return on your money. Other investment vehicles (bonds, commodities, etc.) will start to look more attractive by comparison. Some people may start thinking, "This game isn't looking so good any more. Maybe I should sell up and get out."

Unfortunately this is the beginning of the end. Tap D is starting to flow at an ever faster rate. The moment that happens, more and more people will realise that the game is up. The flow into Tap A will slow. The smarter investors know full well that the quicker they sell, the more cash they can take with them as they leave the market. Tap D will turn into a torrent. The bubble will burst.

Politicians and bankers don't want stock market bubbles to burst

Let's go back a moment to the beginning of the end of a stock bubble, that brief period when prices are just starting to fall but have yet to collapse completely. What will be going through the minds of bankers and politicians? Usually they will think, "The economy is about to collapse... let's try to stop the fall!" They will say things like, "We need the banking system to be healthy so that they can do all that essential lending to business." But hopefully now you should be able to see exactly what the fall is: It is a transition from a state in which investors *incorrectly* think they have great future wealth to one in which they *correctly* realise that they don't have great future wealth. The idea that this transition is a bad thing that needs to be prevented is simply ridiculous. Yet time and time again at the tipping point of stock bubbles bankers and politicians frantically try to prevent it happening. They may try several different strategies; for example, lowering interest rates so that it becomes easier for people to borrow (= create) more money in order to buy more shares. This is an attempt to increase the rate flowing from Tap A. Of course this can only be a temporary "solution". It can only delay the inevitable. It can only serve to prolong and exacerbate the period in which people have delusional ideas about their future wealth.

Conclusion

Unrestricted short-term share dealing on the secondary market is a recipe for economic instability. Discouraging the practice with tax penalties will have only a small cost and huge benefits. Share dealing as a whole could then be taken out of the category of pseudo-investments and moved back into the category of investments where it belongs.

14 The Bloated Financial Sector

You may have noticed that the popularity of the activities listed in the chapters on pseudo-investments has grown enormously since the late seventies / early eighties. This corresponds to a period in which the financial sector as a percentage of the whole economy has grown on a similar scale. This is no coincidence. From the bank's perspective pseudo-investments are every bit as profitable as true investments, and so an expansion of these activities will cause the financial sector to grow. As it grows it will inevitably make more profit and accordingly will pay more in tax to the government. Sadly this fact has led politicians to believe that a large financial sector is good for the economy. The government will see that the financial sector is contributing ever greater sums to the total tax revenue. The politicians have said to themselves, "Look at how successful our financial sector is. Whatever they're up to, let's encourage it!" This is poor logic. By that same argument, if the mafia paid taxes the government should also say, "These tax revenues are massive... this must be an excellent business. Whatever it is they're doing, let's encourage it!"

The problem with the profits from pseudo-investments is that they come from "the rest of us". Pseudo-investments are worse than useless, but due to a variety of illusions, hopefully now revealed, governments and the population at large have been deceived into believing that they are all of great benefit. We have been giving an ever larger fraction of our wealth to the financial sector since the early eighties, and until very recently we've scarcely even noticed anything was going wrong.

One way to visualise our new state of financial affairs is to consider the following representation of money flows in our economy today:

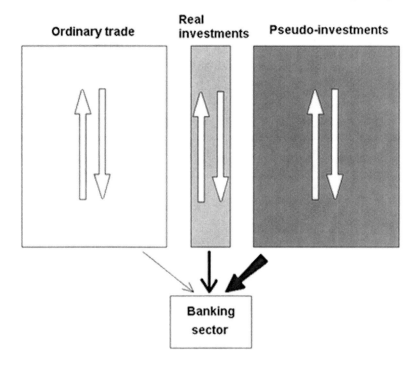

Figure 14-1 The flow of money.

On the left we have ordinary trade, which is people earning money and spending it: I make stuff in my factory, I sell it to other people, they give me money for it, I use that money to buy stuff that they make in their factories etc. The two back and forth arrows represent the flow of money involved in this part of the economy. You will notice a slim arrow leading to the banking sector. This represents the very small amounts of money that banks make from these transactions. Clearly if the transactions are carried out with cash then exactly zero goes to the banks. If cheques or debit cards (not credit cards) are used then a very small processing fee may be payable.

The middle block in the diagram represents money flows involved in *real* investments: I borrow money from the bank to buy a new machine for my factory so that I can make goods more efficiently, I pay back interest on these loans. This sector is smaller than the "ordinary trade" sector but the flow of money to banks is higher. Banks quite justifiably seek interest payments on these loans and so there is a fatter arrow drawn leading from this part of the economy to the banking sector. The bankers involved in these flows are essential. These are the "good" bankers. They need to be highly skilled and will deservedly be well paid.

In a healthy economy the diagram would now be complete. There is no great need for anything else. But sadly our economy has grown an enormous third sector, the pseudo-investment sector. Non-productive investments, private tailgating, government tailgating, mortgages, short-term secondary share dealing, the list goes on. The size of these transactions has grown like a cancer on society since the late seventies / early eighties and all require a continuous stream of interest to be paid to banks. The arrow is the biggest of the three by far. This is why the banking sector is so large. This is why bankers are so rich. It's nothing short of a disaster for the economy.

15 The Private Pensions Casino

The idea of pensions in a barter system, i.e. without money, may seem quite bizarre. We have gotten so accustomed to the modern, money-based concept of pensions that we assume that without money pensions could not exist. But actually money-based pensions are historically the exception, not the rule. Interestingly, though, throughout the past millennia pensions worked just fine in a completely different way.

Pensions throughout history

Let's just take a moment to think about what a pension is and why we need them. We all realise that when we reach old age we can no longer work as efficiently in the production of goods and services, either to consume ourselves or to exchange with other people for whatever we need to get by. The standard way this situation has been dealt with throughout history is via the family. As long as you were fortunate enough to have a loving family, your children would look after you in your later years. They would give you some of their food, shelter etc. There was no need for any legal contract; it was just "the done thing". Note that neither parents nor children were aware of any "savings" going on in this process. The system was completely stable and could work for generation after generation without any "warehouse" being filled up with any goods for later use. Looking at the society as a whole you could simply observe that at all times there were some younger working people donating a fraction of their produce to older retired people.

Now let's consider the introduction of money into this system. Presumably the same scenario could be arranged: You could have a continuous flow of money from younger working people to older retired people. Systems could be devised to enable this to take place. But bizarrely it has not happened. Instead we seem to have evolved a model in the west which involves a kind of "storing things in a warehouse" model of savings.

Now, many people may try to defend our modern pensions system. They may claim that the money saved by people during their working lives needs to be used for "investments". They may claim that alternative systems are too "socialist" and deny us our freedoms. We have objections to both those arguments on several grounds. But first of all let's consider the effects of our modern "money and savings" based pensions system with a story:

Mr Lucky and Mr Unlucky

Consider two people born five years apart. Let's call them Mr Lucky (the older man) and Mr Unlucky. Let us imagine that they are equally conscientious, equally hard working, equally intelligent, equally everything.

Now Mr Lucky starts his working life and starts saving towards his pension. Just by chance this is at the end of a recession when stock prices are low. He's already off to a good start because his early pension's investments are likely to rise nicely.

Five years later Mr Unlucky starts his working life. He does a similar job and saves the same fraction of his income toward his pension. Unfortunately now is the peak of a stock bubble. His early pension's investments will turn out to be a disaster.

For several decades to come both men have investments in the stock market at the same time. Unfortunately Mr Unlucky's fund manager is not as financially savvy as Mr Lucky's. This is not really Mr Unlucky's fault – neither men are financial experts. How can anyone possibly expect your average man in the street to determine the different skill levels of two different fund managers? They can't. Mr Unlucky's fund gradually drifts even further behind Mr Lucky's. But it doesn't stop there...

The fund managers make their choices based on their knowledge of the markets and the economic "fundamentals", i.e. the balance of trade between countries, rates of unemployment, tax laws, political changes, levels of natural resources etc. etc. However, a sizable component of the variability of stock prices is things that no fund manager could be expected to prepare for, like earthquakes, floods, political assassinations, industrial accidents etc. And you've guessed it – the floods and earthquakes just happen to be to the benefit of Mr Lucky's stocks and Mr Unlucky's fund manager's stock selections get badly hit, so his pension fund falls even further behind. But it doesn't stop there...

Now we come to retirement time and would you believe it, Mr Lucky retires at the peak of another bubble and so has a boosted pension pot just when he buys his annuity. And oh dear, Mr Unlucky retires at the depths of a recession so his pension pot is additionally suppressed at the time of purchasing his.

So there you have it – two similar guys doing similar jobs, saving similar fractions of their wages towards their retirements and yet their retirement incomes could be hugely different based entirely on luck. Is that fair? Is that how we want the system to work? Some people find it extremely stressful worrying about their pensions – are they going to be lucky or unlucky? What should they do? Should they just save way more than they really need just in case they're unlucky? Or should they scrimp on their pension contributions hoping they get lucky and then simply carry on working longer if they're unlucky?

Note that there two types of random variability between pensioners. One type is between pensioners of the same age. Let's call this *stock selection variability*. Another type is concerned with the start and end times of pensioners' saving period. Call this *bubble timing variability*. Now bubble timing variability will affect entire age groups of pensioners, some of them having miserable retirements and others having good ones.

Just imagine if you applied the same pensions system in your own home. Imagine you have your old grandma and grandpa living with you. They've both worked hard all their lives. Now at dinnertime you serve Grandma a feast of the finest foods and champagne while you give Grandpa a slice of bread and a glass of water. They say, "What did we do to deserve this?" and you have to remind them that Grandma thought eBay was a great idea and Grandpa liked the Betamax video cassette system (for younger readers – you should know that Betamax was a commercial disaster).

Now you may say that this is simply how life is – if you get lucky then you do better in life, if you're unlucky then you do worse. But that's not true in all aspects of our lives, and people can usually *select* the degree of risk they want to take. If you want to be a professional stock broker then you may get rich or you may go bust; it goes with the territory. People *choose* to be stockbrokers. Nobody who loses on the stock market ever says, "Gee, nobody told me there was any risk involved." But we can choose to take a less risky career. Say you become employed as a plumber. There's not much risk in that. If business gets bad then you can always retrain as something else. There's little chance of ever suddenly having your life savings wiped out as a plumber. So you see there are some choices in our working lives which are inherently risky and some inherently less so. Now when it comes to designing a pension system, is it so obvious that we should select a mechanism so full of risk? We think not. It is possible to design an inherently safer mechanism.

A fairer pensions system

Now the first characteristic we want for a pensions system is that people who save more in their working lives should get more – and roughly speaking if you save twice as much as the average guy in your working life then you should get twice as much in your retirement.

The second characteristic of the system is that people must be forced to save for at least a minimum standard of living in retirement. Now some people may say, "How dare you take away our freedom! It's up to us to individually decide what we save for retirement." But not saving throughout your life puts a blatantly unfair burden on the rest of society when you retire. We can't just stand by and watch you become homeless and starve. We'll be forced to give you a certain minimum standard of living for free. We would also add that the amount we are *forced* to save for retirement will be very small. Just enough so that you could have a bare minimum quality of life.

A system to achieve all these things is the following:

The government invent a new type of tax (but of course we don't want to call it a tax!), call this *compulsory elderly-support*. Say its X%. This is the minimum. People can optionally also put whatever extra they want into the elderly-support system. The continuous flow of elderly-support money that comes in from workers is used to pay money to the retired. Note that this is all happening at one instant – there is no pretence that some investment is being put in

191

storage for future use. It's plain and simply workers-now-support-retired-people-now.

So the next question is how to apportion the money – this is where we need to do a little mathematical jiggery pokery. The money is not distributed evenly among retired people, instead it is (roughly speaking) distributed in proportion to the amount of money those retired people fed into the elderly-support system during their working lives. The maths required to achieve this is not trivial, but it is certainly doable.

So what are the advantages of this system?

- Nobody is being forced to predict the stock market. People who save similar amounts will be similarly comfortable in their retirements.

- If a country develops well and has a boom then the retired population will automatically benefit from the boom.

- If the country has a recession then retired people will take their share of the burden rather than requiring an unbearably large fraction of the now-poorer nations' GDP.

- The whole system will be far more predictable for pensioners, workers and government.

16 Land Ownership and Mortgages

In recent decades free market economists in the west have promoted the idea of mass home ownership. They often insisted that owning your own home was some sort of right, something that people should have the freedom to do. They have assumed that, without regulation and without the government interference of "social" housing mechanisms, the free market will result in a state where most people will own their own homes. Indeed in many western countries home ownership appears to have increased markedly in recent decades. Sadly this increase has been part of the cause of the crash of 2007/8.

This chapter aims to show how the modern concept of mass home ownership in industrialised countries simply cannot be made to work in a way that is simultaneously equitable and economically stable without substantial modifications to our current system. To help illustrate exactly why this is so we shall need the help of a thought experiment, but before we get to that we must first be clear about the main cost of housing.

Most of the cost of housing is in fact the cost of land

If all land were somehow magically free of charge then the average annual cost of housing would be approximately:

$$M + C / Y$$

Where

M = the average annual maintenance costs (e.g. roof repairs)

C = the cost of building a house in the first place (bricks and mortar and labour)

Y = the number of years the house will last.

This theoretical housing cost (with free land) is only a fraction of what most people in the industrialised world are actually paying. The difference is the cost of the land.

A thought experiment about land

Imagine that a few hundred people are placed on a desert island where there is limited space. There is no way to get off the island; they will all be living there for the rest of their lives. They will want to divide up the land so that each person or family can build houses. Undoubtedly not everyone will have the same preference for land. For example one person may love fishing and so be very keen to be by the sea; another may love playing tennis so they would be keen to have a large flat piece of land; someone else may like sitting at home reading books and not really care much about how much space they get; others may simply want to live close to wherever their friends are. Imagine that on day one they all gather together to discuss what mechanism they should use for distributing the land fairly. Let us examine a few options...

Drawing lots

First of all, how about simply dividing the land into equal-sized areas and then draw lots? At first glance this seems eminently fair. How could anyone complain? The problem is that it is a sub-optimal solution. The keen tennis player could, by chance, end up on the side of a hill while a keen hill-walker ends up on a perfectly flat piece of land. Clearly both would be unhappy with this outcome. Surely we can do better…

The committee

Another possible solution is to elect a committee who will distribute the land according to the people's needs. This could be seen as the "communist" solution. If the members of the committee have a good grasp of the needs of all the individuals in the population then they may stand a chance of coming up with a reasonable solution. But above a certain threshold of population size it quickly becomes impossible for the members to truly know all the people's needs. What they will be forced to do then is formulate sets of rules about who should get what pieces of land. This is where the trouble starts. Devising sets of rules about real-world human problems is fiendishly difficult. The number of factors to consider for each person is liable to be so large that a rule-based system is doomed to produce significant unfairness. Surely we can do better…

Free market renting

Keen free-marketeers might step in at this point and say, "Leave it to the free market. The free market is perfect for sorting out this kind of problem." The idea is that people who are willing and able to pay the most should get the best land and people willing to pay the least should get the smaller or less desirable plots. But given that all the people were placed on the land at the same time, nobody owns any land to start with – so to whom could anyone pay any rent?

Indeed this problem would still exist to this day in the real world were it not for some sort of bootstrapping mechanism to get things started. Historically by far the most common way people got going with land ownership was to claim land by force, or at least the threat of force. But if we were to start over again with modern, civilised people wishing to distribute land fairly without violence, how should we begin? Luckily there is a solution:

A free market solution would be the following:

1. Instigate "Desert Island Land Rental Ltd", a company that will own all the land on the island.

2. Make all the islanders equal shareholders.

3. Allow all the islanders to bid a rent for whatever plots of land they desire.

4. Rent each plot to the highest bidder.

5. Distribute the money received equally among the islanders (shareholders).

This way everyone gets to have an equal share of the *value* of the land but the precise way the land gets distributed is then determined according to a combination of people's desires and ability to pay rent.

An interesting consequence of this process would be that some people would get their land for free. If someone just happened to pay an amount for their plot that was exactly equal to the average price paid for all the plots then their dividend payment from Desert Island Land Rental Ltd would exactly match their bid. People who bid more than average for the best bits of land would still be out of pocket; they would be net contributors. Those who bid less than the average and lived in the poorer quality or smaller patches of land would actually get paid to live on their patch!

At this point we can imagine some readers thinking to themselves that this is a crazy, mixed-up system. People being paid to live on certain patches of land? Surely some mistake!

Is the concept of some people being paid to live on their land really so strange? Some points to consider...

If it were just *two* families on a (very small) desert island, and there were clearly just two patches of land suitable for house building, one clearly nicer than the other, how would they resolve that between them without a fight? In that case it seems obvious that the family most keen to get the nicer plot would agree to give some sort of compensation to the other. If this principle makes sense for two families, why not apply it to society as a whole?

Another thing to consider when pondering the seemingly odd concept of some people being paid to live on their land is the fact that even with our current real-world system, for some people land is a source of income rather than an expense. Anyone who owns lots of land can charge rent to others. Indeed in the real world the rate of flow of money being used to rent or buy land is exactly equal to the rate of flow of money being *received* by other people for renting/selling land. The difference between the status in the thought experiment and the status in the real world is that in the real world some private *individuals* are deemed to own land. It is individuals who can receive rent for any excess land beyond that required for their personal use.

Any land that happens to be owned by the state and rented out will earn money for the state and therefore subsidise tax income. Income from *this* rent is effectively being "paid" to everyone in society, in a way not too dissimilar to that described in the Desert Island Land Rental company example.

There are clear advantages of this system over the lottery and the committee: As long as he is willing and able to pay, the tennis player can get his large flat piece of land, the hill walker can get his patch on the side of a hill, the fisherman can get his land by the sea and so on. What's more, if someone cares more about the ability to buy goods than having lots of land then they can opt for a small patch and be paid by the rest of the community for enabling them have more space. They can then use this income for whatever it is that they prefer to have, perhaps more food, wine, nicer clothes etc.

It should be noted that the rental system described here is just a crude outline. In practice there would need to be measures to allow for people to move from one place to another and to allow for population growth. Boundaries between plots of land may need to change occasionally, new homes built, old homes demolished etc.

The free market with purchasing as an option

The rental system seems to solve a lot of problems, but some people may prefer to *own* their land. So instead of paying a certain fraction of their produce on a continuous basis, they would prefer to pay a lump sum at some point and then own that land, with nothing further to pay, in perpetuity. Let us now consider this option in a little detail with some more thought experiments.

Let's start off with the example of the two families on the very small desert island. Again one plot of land is clearly nicer than the other and again let's consider the negotiations about who gets to live on the nicer part. What is the likelihood that the deal struck would be a purchase agreement rather than a rental one? If the difference in quality/quantity between the two patches of land is very small then it is perfectly possible that the family willing to put up with the smaller piece of land may accept a one-off collection of goods in permanent payment. But if the difference in quality/quantity is more substantial then we run into a problem. The families will be living on their respective plots for decades to come and so the perceived value of living on the nicer plot over an entire lifetime will be enormous. Most likely the difference in perceived value will be greater than the entire collection of goods that either family *currently* posses. Purchasing is thus very unlikely to be able to occur.

Now let us expand the island to have more people. Say there are 100 families and they are employing the Desert Island Land Rent or Purchase Ltd" model, i.e. they are all shareholders in a company that can choose to either rent or sell plots of land. Now in order for one family to purchase rather than rent their land they still would be unlikely to have a collection of goods that the land company would accept as preferable to a rental agreement. But now there is a possible alternative. It may be the case that the sum of all the current property of a *collection* of islanders would be deemed equivalent to a rental agreement. So if a family can persuade a collection of other islanders to lend them enough goods in return for repayment with interest, then a purchase agreement could go ahead. We can sum up this scenario as follows:

In general, in order for land purchase to be viable, a substantial collection of goods needs to be amassed. This collection will often be far larger than an individual has in their current possession. Thus the only way a purchase can go ahead is for that person to *borrow* goods in return for an agreement to repay with interest.

Hopefully now you should be able to see that the number of people who can purchase land at any one time should be limited to a small fraction of the total population. Any attempt to have too much land purchasing should run into a problem of lack of available savings. We say "should" because actually there is one way round the problem – in earlier chapters we saw that fractional reserve banking enabled borrowing to take place against the will of society. If a system of fractional reserve banking is in place then the rate of new land sales can rise above what it otherwise would be, via the mechanism of inflation. We can summarise the situation as follows:

> In any period in which the number of landowners increases at too fast a rate the money supply will be forced to grow fast, devaluing the existing currency: a perfect recipe for a land/housing bubble.
>
> In a fixed or nearly fixed money supply system like full reserve banking, there would simply not be sufficient savings for this rate of mortgage lending to come about.

Income from owned land – another problem

Another issue that emerges from land ownership is something known as the "Mathew Effect" or more simply the "the rich get richer effect". Once a private individual becomes the owner of more land than they require for their own immediate needs, they can rent out their excess. The income from this process could then be used to purchase more land which can be rented out and so on in a never-ending spiral. Left unchecked this process would inevitably lead to gross inequalities in wealth among the population.

You could argue that the Mathew Effect is simply a built-in feature of capitalism. Anyone that manufactures a successful product can use any resulting profits to build a factory and manufacture another successful product and so on and so on. But the key difference here is that one process is productive and the other is not. Rewarding people for coming up with good product ideas and having the skills to manufacture them at a price people can afford benefits society as a whole. Gaining ever more land on the basis of owning existing land benefits only the landowner to the *detriment* of the rest of society.

If the tax system is rigged such that land ownership is a more attractive means of making money than working in other industries then this has terrible social consequences both in terms of unfair wealth distribution and bubble promotion.

Environmental consequences

With the desert island land rental model if someone thinks to themselves, "I'm not greedy, I want a simple life. I'll just work a few short hours per day (enough to cover my personal needs) and have a modest piece of land and a simple house", then of course they will be able to do that. Their land will cost them nothing, or even less than nothing. They can do a small amount of work and live frugally. That plan may not be to everyone's tastes, but some people do think that way and environmentally it's good news – the more people think that way, the less of the earth's resources we will consume and the less carbon we'll put into the atmosphere.

Contrast this with what happens under our current system. A person with that exact same mindset is virtually barred from carrying out their plan. Under the current system, people are born with precisely zero entitlement to any land at all. They are effectively born owing a lifetime's rent to other private individuals for any land they want to live on. They are effectively compelled to earn the money to pay that rent by doing considerable amounts of work, consuming scarce resources and putting carbon into the atmosphere in the process. They will have to do this work throughout the major part of their entire lifespan. The environmental consequences are disastrous.

Conclusion

Widespread land ownership by private individuals is problematic in a wide variety of ways and would simply not happen in a true free market. The cheerleading and subsidising of mass home ownership by Margaret Thatcher, Ronald Reagan, George Bush and other (self-proclaimed) free marketeers was a significant contributor to the current economic crisis.

17 Restless Bandits and Competition

Many economists seem to believe that every problem in economics can be solved by removing regulation and "letting the markets decide". Other people disagree and will use a variety of hand-waving arguments to explain why that's sub-optimal. This chapter will consider a certain well-analysed, statistical conundrum that has a striking parallel to a problem in economics, and its study could remove the need for some of these hand-waving arguments and replace them with something closer to mathematical proof. The conundrum is a variation of the "multi-armed bandit problem" – but before we explain what it is, or its solution, we'd better explain the problem in economics that it so neatly parallels.

The problem is: Who should make new Product X? Communists might say, "Let's have an expert government committee choose a single company (Y) and only allow that company to make X". The free marketeers would say, "Let multiple companies (A, B, C, D and E) make X and the market will decide which is the best and let the others go bust – and for goodness sake, don't let the government interfere with this process!"

Now we will introduce the statistical conundrum. It's called the "multi-armed bandit" problem:

The casino owner and the screwdriver

Imagine you have a collection of one-armed bandits (slot machines) in a casino. Each one has a certain payout rate, which corresponds to the percentage of the money paid into it, that it will pay out in the long run. In real casinos this is often set at something like 80–90%, but imagine that this particular model of one-armed bandit can be set to any predefined payout rate (0% to 100%) by turning a dial inside the machine that the casino owner can set with a screwdriver. Now let's say that one night the casino owner comes in and sets each mchine to a different payout rate. You arrive the following morning with a big bag of coins. You are determined to spend the whole day playing on these bandits. You have complete freedom to choose which ones you play on; you are allowed to switch from one to another at will. Now the question is: What is your strategy for selecting bandits such that you come home with the greatest winnings? Or, more likely, the least losses.

One possible solution: Put 50 coins in each of the bandits in order to make an *estimate* of their *true payout rates*. Then stick to the one that appears to have the highest rate for the rest of the day.

At this point it is essential to be quite clear about the difference between the ***estimated payout rate*** and ***the true payout rate***.

The true payout rate is the rate set (with the screwdriver) by the casino owner. This is the theoretical rate given an infinite amount of plays. The estimated payout rate is your estimate of the true payout rate based on the evidence of your trials so far. If you have had very few trials then your estimate can only be a rough guess. Your guess will gradually become more accurate the more trials you have, but in practice you can never become completely certain.

This "50 coin" solution is certainly better than simply selecting the bandits at random but can be mathematically proven to be sub-optimal, i.e. there are known strategies that will lead to greater winnings. The problem with the 50 coin strategy is that if two bandits paid out rather good, but very similar amounts, than it may not be very clear which is better. It may be more profitable to continue playing these two for a greater number of trials to gain more accuracy in your estimated payout rates before selecting which is the best one. The problem illustrates what is known as the *exploitation–exploration dilemma*. The "exploration" refers to the effort exploring which bandit may be the best (e.g. the 50 coin trial at the start) and the "exploitation" refers to exploiting your current knowledge, i.e. simply repeatedly playing the bandit which you estimate is the best.

This conundrum is rather analogous to the process of choosing companies to make products in a free market. The bandits are like the companies, the payouts are like the goods they make and the gambler is like the public, choosing the "company" that produces the best "goods". At the start of the process the public does not know for sure who can make the best version of Product X so they may try a variety of them. After a while the different companies start to gain different reputations. The reputations are like the estimated payout rates.

The known bad companies will cease to be tried (= "go bust") while the still-possibly-best will get tried some more.

Restless bandits

Now there is one more complication that needs to be added to the standard multi-armed bandit problem to make it even more analogous to real-life business. There is a variation called the "restless bandit problem" where the payout rates are not fixed but rather evolve over time. This is more like a real company where the management and employees will change over time. Their manufacturing equipment may wear out, break or become redundant and a host of other things may happen that will change the ability of the company to produce good products. Now in the *restless* bandit problem it is essential to do more "exploration" than in the case of the standard multi-armed bandit problem. You would never want to entirely give up trying a previously poor performing bandit because it may have now evolved into a better performing bandit.

It can be mathematically proven that for the restless bandit problem the 50 coin strategy is even more sub-optimal than is the case for the fixed bandit problem. There is too little "exploration". It is sub-optimal for two reasons:

1. You may be mistaken in your estimate of which one has the highest true payout rate.

2. The true best bandit may change over time.

This result has important implications for free marketeers. It proves that the free market is sub-optimal. A free market acts like the "too little exploration" strategy. In a free market companies that fall short of producing the best goods tend to go bust even if they only fall short by a small margin. Also companies occasionally go bust for essentially random reasons unconnected with their underlying ability to make goods cheaply. For example, a company can go bust as a consequence of a one-in-a-hundred-years hurricane that disrupts a key supplier. Obviously when a company goes bust it can never be "tried" again; it doesn't get a second chance. The surviving companies will then tend to grow, filling the void, and dominate the market. In the absence of counteracting forces, this process is liable to be one-way, resulting in a monopoly. Once a company grows very large and dominates a market, it will naturally benefit from a variety of economies of scale. It will be able to negotiate harder with both suppliers and distributors. What's more, it can use its market power to make exclusivity deals with various other companies in the chain from raw materials to shop window. All of these things mean that there is no longer a level playing field between the company and any new small rivals.

Monopolies: okay at first – but then...

When a monopoly first emerges it may well do so because it was actually a well-run, efficient company beating its competition into bankruptcy with superior products or services. However, armed with such advantages over any new competition that may arise later, the evolutionary process is now weakened. The company's incentive to remain good value is reduced, so over the years problems can emerge. If the management retire or move on and are replaced by some less skilled people the company may now not be so efficient, but by exploiting its monopolistic advantage it may well be able to hold on to its dominance. Society can end up with an inefficient supplier and little choice.

These factors make the "too little exploration" strategy in economics even more sub-optimal when compared to the restless bandit domain. It's as if as soon as we make up our minds and settle on the bandit that we think is best, it gradually reduces its payout rate.

In any exploration–exploitation dilemma it is, of course, quite possible to make the mistake of doing *too much* exploration. In the extreme that would be like playing all of the bandits equally often regardless of their observed payout rates. This can easily be proven to be sub-optimal too. So there is a balance between exploration and exploitation to be struck.

Conclusion

In the real world there are many things that could be done to make sure that there is enough "exploration" in an economy, some of which are already in place to a greater or lesser extent in many countries. We would recommend the following:

- laws to discourage or prevent the setting up of exclusive supply or distribution channels
- lower levels of regulation of smaller companies compared to larger ones
- lower taxes for smaller companies compared to larger ones.

You might point out that some of these suggestions are already in place in some countries, but hopefully the analogy of the restless bandit problem a) gives some mathematical support for these kind of policies and b) proves unequivocally that free market fundamentalism is sub-optimal.

18 A Recipe for a More Stable Economy

Hopefully this book has now made it clear what features of our current system lead to economic instability. We are now in a position to design a new system to reduce such evils as positive feedback, Ponzi dynamics, pseudo-investments, excess unemployment and crazy stock prices.

Reduce unnecessary lending and borrowing

In Chapter 4 we showed how Ponzi dynamics are built into many forms of savings. Given this fact, the first ingredient of a stable economy is to minimise all lending and borrowing that is of no benefit to the economy as a whole. This will require a radical undoing of the way modern economies have embraced these practices in recent decades. In order to get this idea accepted, it is helpful to appreciate that so many of these arrangements are just very recent inventions. They should be seen as an experiment that has failed. The "radical" idea of curtailing them should be seen as no more and no less than reverting to how things have mostly worked since antiquity. Let's consider these unnecessary activities in turn:

Less borrowing to consume

This very modern experiment of encouraging widespread use of credit cards to purchase so many goods hampers productive investment. The advantages of this practice are outweighed by the disadvantages and so should be reduced to a minimum. Borrowing to consume should go back to being seen as a last resort when something has "gone wrong". The precise mechanism for reducing the popularity of this form of borrowing is perhaps debatable. One step would be to eliminate credit cards altogether. If someone really wants to borrow money then they can visit their bank manager in person to explain their predicament. If the manager agrees then a good old-fashioned loan can go ahead.

Less mortgages

Chapter 16 showed how widespread private mortgages simply cannot occur in any reasonable way. We need to move toward a model much closer to, or equivalent to, nationalised land ownership with renting being the predominant mechanism of putting a roof over your head. Any land-related taxes must also be designed so as to eliminate or control the Mathew (rich get richer) effect.

Reconsider private pensions

Chapter 15 showed how the entire concept of attempting to build up a fund during your working life that you can live off in your old age is a modern experiment that is being revealed as a dismal failure at the time of writing. Pensions need to work on the basis of "working people *now* support retired people *now*". There is no need for any "savings" to be involved.

A much reduced financial sector

Given that the financial sector currently makes most of its profits on the back of these kinds of unproductive borrowing/lending, the size of the sector without them will be far smaller. Any transition to such a system will involve a lot of bankers having to retrain or start up their own non-finance-related companies.

A less elastic monetary system

We need to reform the monetary system, either to something more akin to 100% reserve banking or, alternatively, a rebalanced fractional reserve system where the monetary base is a *far* higher proportion of the money supply. New, debt-free money will need to be printed for this purpose – *without* the convoluted mechanism of purchasing bonds.

No money creation for non-productive purposes

Whatever the monetary system, it is essential that money not be *created* for non-productive purposes. In particular, money must not be created for purchasing any of the following:

- land/residential property
- shares in the secondary market
- commodities
- derivatives.

Anyone that wants to invest in these items must do so with pre-existing money.

Discourage short-term share ownership

Chapter 13 showed exactly how the popularity of short-term share ownership inevitably leads to wildly fluctuating share prices in a way that does nothing but harm to the economy. Mechanisms to discourage this practice must be introduced. We suggest a tax on share transactions which start high when the shares have been held for a very short time and then diminishes as the duration of ownership increases.

Whatever system is used, its effectiveness should be measured by listening to the "water-cooler conversations". If people are discussing earning from long-term dividends then all is well. If people are still discussing making money from short-term share price changes then not enough is being done.

Prevent governments from borrowing

Chapter 12 showed how countries are analogous to super-large companies that do not need to borrow externally in order to invest.

This rule only applies to countries of a reasonable size. If you are a small island in the pacific there may be a case for borrowing in some circumstances.

The transition from our current state

Making the transition from our current economic system to the one prescribed would be a major and complex undertaking to put it mildly. Inevitably there will be winners and losers. The details of how to make the transition in the most equitable and least painful way would perhaps take up a large book or even several large books on their own. You wouldn't expect that fixing the world economy was going to be easy, would you?

Acknowledgements

During my economics research I have come across some great independent thinkers, most notably Professor Steve Keen who saw the crash coming a mile off and is in my opinion one of the most important economists in the world today. My ideas have also been influenced to varying degrees by Michael Hudson, Peter Schiff, Robert Shiller, William Black, Jim Rogers, Marc Faber, Janet Tavakoli, Mike Shedlock, and Karl Denninger.

I would also like to add a special word for Max Keiser and Stacy Herbert for hosting the most entertaining and challenging alternative economics programs on television.

I would like to thank the following people for giving me invaluable feedback during the preparation of this book: Christopher Foster, Russell Bradshaw, Ben Dyson, Craft Holtz, Mikhail Kotuzhansky, Pierre Cottez, Leona O'Brien, Sally Darcy, Jonny Friend, David Foot, Nick Powell, Karen Mellor, Eva Osborne, Jeff Rollason, Daniel Mason and Bernadette Barrett.

About the Author

Michael Reiss obtained a degree in physics and followed it up with a PhD in neural networks. He then went on to a career in artificial intelligence, during which he became world champion at programming the ancient oriental strategy game of Go (Shanghai 1999). Michael's interest in economics was first sparked during a spell as a programmer at Chase Manhattan Bank, and he has been researching heterodox economics since 2007. He lives in London with his girlfriend and daughter.

Index

CPSIA information can be obtained at www.ICGtesting.com
Printed in the USA
245053LV00015B/96/P